The Continental Div ide:
Racing Towards Reconciliation

The Continental Div ide:

Racing Towards Reconciliation

Kandis Heckler

2008

The Continental Div ide:
Racing Towards Reconciliation

Request for all books, plays, DVDs, conference schedule:
Agape Productions Inc.
P.O. Box 4385
Wheaton, Illinois 60189
www.agapeproductionsinc.com
agapeproductions@sbcglobal.net

ISBN: 0-9670555-3-9
ISBN-13: 978-0967055534

Visit www.booksurge.com to order additional copies.

The Continental Div ide:
Racing Towards Reconciliation

The Continental Div ide:
Racing Towards Reconciliation

Contents

Acknowledgements

TO MY DADDY, JESUS:
To my Heavenly Father, thank you for the inspiration, wisdom and the words and for allowing Jesus to be the best example of a man who reconciled Himself with the world.

TO MY BELOVED GIFTS FROM GOD:
To my children, thank you for being precious gifts from the Lord and allowing me to share my time with you with the rest of the world.

TO MY MOMMY AND DADDY:
Thank you for giving me a solid biblical foundation for my faith.

TO TAMMY BARLEY:
Thank you for yet another excellent job on editing.

IN MEMORY OF:
Carla Denise Cobb who was a great woman of faith who taught me how precious life is.

Foreword

You are all sons of God through faith in Christ Jesus, for all of you who were baptized into Christ have clothed yourselves with Christ. There is neither Jew nor Greek, slave nor free, male nor female, for you are all one in Christ Jesus. If you belong to Christ, then you are Abraham's seed, and heirs according to the promise.

-Galatians 3:26-29

Writing a book on racial reconciliation was one of the most difficult assignments the Lord has given me. I wasn't excited about revisiting all of the prejudicial and discriminatory experiences I've endured in my lifetime. I simply did not want to recall any of those unpleasant occurrences.

How many of us know that when God calls you to do something, you don't wait around for a second warning? So in submission and with a healthy dosage of trepidation thrown in for good measure I chose to obey God. So here it is, my attempt to be used for His glory.

While compiling the research and studying, I realized the issue of reconciliation isn't as difficult as we all make it out to be. If we were all operating with the knowledge of what Galatians 3:26-29 means this book and others like it would not be necessary. According to that Scripture we are all adopted into the family of God if we are true believers. And just like my adopted children have the same rights and privileges as my biological children and will share in my inheritance equally, it is the same with God and us.

Our unity in Christ transcends any ethnicity, religious, socioeconomic status, gender and any additional distinctions we assign to ourselves. Christ died for us all. We are all one in Him. If we belong to Christ we are Abraham's seed and heirs according to the promise. Wow! What a heritage we have. And it is available to us. All we have to do is ask.

When conception began for this book, I asked the Lord to give me an anointing for this one unlike any of my previous works. This was my first nonfiction book, and I had to rely on wisdom from Him to complete it. With the other books, I was able to use my overactive imagination. This one required a tremendous amount of discipline, studying and research. Frankly I wasn't really thrilled about it. Another thing I asked of Him was that He tell me what to write so this book would assist its readers with the healing process. And the Holy Spirit, as He always does, graciously reminded me that healing needed to begin with the author of the book. It wasn't until I began to recall all my personal experiences that I realized that for a majority of my life (and may I add, I am not that old) I have been harboring strong feelings of resentment against my Caucasian sisters and brothers in the Lord.

I was angry at them because I perceived they thought that since they were born into Caucasian ancestry they were entitled to more privileges than the rest of us. In reflection, wasn't I just as wrong in my perception of them as those who were perpetrating discrimination against me based on my race? The Holy Spirit will reveal things to you if you ask Him.

So guess what I did? I repented and asked the Lord to forgive me of my trespasses. And He did. He removed my sins as far as the east is from the west.

As I sought to publish this book, I asked for feedback from several publishing companies who rejected the manuscript. The consensus among them was the material was too controversial and didn't fit the image of their company. If that isn't confirmation about the long journey ahead of us I don't know what is. I just know whenever God tells us to do something we'd better do it. So it is with humility and a broken and contrite spirit that I offer this book to all of you who strive daily to race towards reconciliation.

So on your mark, get ready, get set, go....

Chapter One

A Very Personal Inventory

Before we get started, please take a moment to complete the first few pages in this book as a personal inventory by recording some of your thoughts about experiences with African Americans. If you are an African American, record your thoughts about your first experience with a Caucasian.

What was your first experience interacting with a person from another race or culture like?

Were there any misconceptions about the individual that were dispelled or reinforced?

Were there any surprises about the individual?

Share an incident of conflict you may have had with an individual of a different race or culture.

Was the incident based on a perceived racial problem or a misunderstanding?

How was the situation handled?

Do you feel it was handled properly?

How could you have handled it differently?

What annoys you the most about another race?

What one question would you ask a person from a different race if you could ask anything without offending them?

Would you ever date a person from a different race? Please explain.

Would you marry a person from a different race? Please explain.

Would you allow your child to marry a person from a different race? Please explain.

As a Caucasian, do you feel you are granted special privileges? Please explain.

As a Caucasian, do you feel superior or inferior to the rest of the population? Please explain.

As an African American, do you feel you are always discriminated against? Please explain.

As an African American, do you feel you should be financially compensated for slavery? Please explain.

As an African American, when you walk into a crowded room dominated by Caucasian males, what's your first reaction? Please explain.

As a Caucasian walking into a crowded room of African-American men, what is your first reaction? Please explain.

Would you invite an African-American person to your church? Please explain.

Would you ever consider attending an African-American church? Please explain.

Would you invite an individual of a different race out to dinner? Please explain.

Would you visit them at their home? Please explain.

Would you invite them to your house? Please explain.

Are interracial children black or white? Please explain.

Would you ever consider adopting an African-American child? Please explain.

Would you consider volunteering in an under-served African-American community? Please explain.

Would you consider moving into a predominately African-American community? Please explain.

List ten adjectives you feel describe African Americans.
1.
2.
3.
4.
5.
6.
7.

8.
9.
10.

List ten stereotypes associated with African Americans.

1.
2.
3.
4.
5.
6.
7.
8.
9.
10.

List ten adjectives you feel describe Caucasians.

1.
2.
3.
4.
5.
6.
7.
8.
9.
10.

List ten stereotypes associated with Caucasians.

1.
2.
3.
4.
5.
6.
7.
8.
9.
10.

Would you vote for an African-American president? Please explain.

Would you hire an African American to work for your company? Please explain.

Would you hire an African American as the CEO of your company? Please explain.

Do you believe in affirmative action? Please explain.

Would you allow an African American to babysit your child? Please explain.

Would you allow an African American the use of your summer home? Please explain.

Just For Fun

Let's see just how much you know about African-American culture. Please circle the correct response.

1. **What is CP time?**
   a. **A time zone in Alaska**
   b. **Colored people arriving late**
   c. **A computer program**
2. **What is Mickey D's?**
   a. **A man who wants to remain anonymous**
   b. **Mickey Mouse's cousin**
   c. **McDonald's**
3. **What does the phrase "she is the bomb" mean?**
   a. **The place will blow up in one minute**
   b. **A woman who thinks she is a gift**
   c. **An acronym for "bring our money, brother"**
4. **How long does an African-American church service last?**
   a. **Until 1:00 p.m.**
   b. **Until 2:00 p.m.**
   c. **Until the Holy Spirit ends it**
5. **What does the word "diss" mean?**
   a. **To disrespect or be disrespected**
   b. **To give someone a hug**
   c. **To owe someone money**
6. **What was "Roots"?**
   a. **A procedure needed at the dentist**
   b. **A mathematical equation**
   c. **A television program**
7. **What is an Oreo?**
   a. **A cookie**
   b. **A black person who "acts white"**
   c. **Both of the above**
8. **What does the word "Tommie" mean?**
   a. **A clothing item**
   b. **A new hair cut**
   c. **A friend named Thomas**
9. **What does a typical African-American Thanksgiving meal consist of?**
   a. **Sushi and tofu**
   b. **Steak and lobster**
   c. **Turkey, cornbread dressing, greens, sweet potato pie**
10. **What is a homeboy?**
    a. **A boy with a home**
    b. **An African-American man**

    c. A clothing designer
11. What is an extension?
    a. A long telephone cord
    b. A phone number
    c. Hair
    d. All the above
12. What does "chillin'" mean?
    a. A country in South America
    b. A spicy stew
    c. Relaxing
13. What is the Soul Train?
    a. The Metra line in Chicago
    b. A slave code for "heaven"
    c. A syndicated television program
14. What is FUBU?
    a. A clothing line
    b. An acronym "for us by us"
    c. Both of the above
15. What are favorite musical choices for African Americans?
    a. Rap
    b. Classical
    c. Interests are varied depending on individual taste
16. What is the standard curfew time for African-American children?
    a. 10:00 p.m.
    b. At their own discretion
    c. Before the street lights come on
17. What month do we celebrate African-American history?
    a. June
    b. August
    c. February
18. What are chitterlings?
    a. A 1960s singing group
    b. Pig intestines
    c. Someone who talks incessantly
19. What is another word for an "evangelistic outreach" in the black community?
    a. Revival
    b. Tent meeting
    c. Vacation Bible school
20. What is a dog?
    a. A four legged animal
    b. An endearing name for an African-American man
    c. Both of the above
21. What are the colors of the African-American flag?
    a. Red, white, blue
    b. Red, green, white

c. Red, green, black

22. What is the name of the Negro National Anthem?

a. The Star Spangled Banner

b. Lift Every Voice and Sing

c. We Shall Overcome

23. Who provided the best example of racial reconciliation?

a. Ghandi

b. Martin Luther King Jr.

c. Jesus Christ

Word Association Game

Directions: Review the word on your left and write the first word that comes to your mind on the right.

Democrats
Homeless
Public aid recipient
Affirmative action
Capital punishment
Gang banger
Jesse Jackson
U.S. Open
Basketball
PGA
Wall Street
Single mother
Immigration
Reparations
Nation of Islam
Al Sharpton
O. J. Simpson
AIDS
Illiterate
Public school
Police brutality
Ivy League
Ritalin
Drug addiction
Crime rate
Gentrification
Billionaire
White House
Wealthy
Stock options
Redlining
Capitalist

Tax evasion
Nazi
Africa
Urban renewal
Intelligent
Disciples
Poverty
Homeowner
College graduate

Fact or Fiction

Directions: Read each statement below and decide whether it is fact or fiction. Write the corresponding answer.

1. **Caucasians are intellectually superior to African Americans.**
2. **African-American men are more likely to be incarcerated than Caucasian men.**
3. **Single-parent homes are disproportionately comprised of African-American women.**
4. **African-American males are more likely to commit violent crimes than Caucasian men.**
5. **Caucasians have more economic power than African Americans.**
6. **Policemen are twice as likely to stop an African-American male driver as a Caucasian male.**
7. **An African American is more likely to be monitored by security in a department store.**
8. **A Caucasian middle-aged man carrying a brief case through airport security usually will be interrogated.**
9. **The rate of college graduation at Harvard for African Americans is 90 percent.**
10. **Nine out of ten African-American high school graduates will attend college sometime in their lifetime.**
11. **Five of the Fortune 500 companies in the United States are owned by African Americans.**
12. **There have been two African-American Noble Peace Prize winners.**
13. **There are four African-American National Basketball Association owners.**
14. **There have been two African-American space shuttle astronauts in NASA history.**
15. **There are more than twenty African-American female pilots for commercial airliners in the United States.**
16. **There are nine African-American state senators.**
17. **An African-American female ran for president of the United States in the 1960s.**
18. **An African American is the second wealthiest according to the Forbes Magazine of 2008.**

19. There are country clubs located in the U.S. where African-American men are prohibited.
20. The majority of African-American boys under age six are hyperactive and in need of Ritalin.
21. Some African-American single-parent women are very strong and aggressive.
22. Historically the majority of African Americans vote Democratic.
23. Statistically there are more African Americans on welfare than any other minority.
24. In the United States, the percentage of millionaires of African-American descent is 15.5 percent.
25. By the time they enter high school, two out of four African-American males will have an altercation with law enforcement.
26. Five out of ten African-American men are incarcerated by their twenty-fifth birthday.
27. The news media accurately portrays African Americans.
28. The murder rate of African Americans within their own community exceeds the national average for murder in other communities.
29. Louis Farrakhan is the national spokesman for the African-American community.
30. Jesse Jackson ran for president of the United States.
31. The military always separated enlisted blacks from whites in the early 1900s.
32. The Civil War was fought in part because of racial hostilities.
33. AIDS originated in Africa.
34. There were no reported cases of housing discrimination in the United States in 2002.

A Moment of Truth—For African Americans

Directions: Complete each sentence.

What annoys me the most about white people is...

I wish white people would not...

White people are notorious for...

White people think they are...

If it wasn't for white people the world would...

White people are always complaining about...

My greatest phobia concerning white people is...

If I could trade places with a white person for a day I would...

White people can never relate to how...

My greatest needs from white people are...

If I could say anything about white people without offending them I would say...

In a perfect world there would be no...

One thing I wish white people would do is...

We are misunderstood by white people concerning...

The best advice my mother gave me about white people was...

When I was a child I thought that white people were...

If black people ruled the world it would be...

If I needed a blood transfusion from a white person I would...

I feel black people should or should not receive reparations because...

Being black in this society makes me feel...

I wish white people would stop blaming everything on...

A Moment of Truth—For Caucasians

Directions: Complete each sentence.

What annoys me the most about black people is...

I wish black people would not...

Black people are notorious for...

Black people think they are...

If it wasn't for black people the world would...

Black people are always complaining about...

My greatest phobia concerning black people is...

If I could trade places with a black person for a day I would...

Black people can never relate to how...

My greatest needs from black people are...

If I could say anything about black people without offending them I would say...

In a perfect world there would be no...

One thing I wish black people would do is...

We are misunderstood by black people concerning...

The best advice my mother gave me about black people was...

When I was a child I thought black people were...

If black people ruled the world it would be...

If I needed a blood transfusion from a black person I would...

I feel black people should or should not receive reparations because...

Being white in this society makes me feel...

I wish black people would stop blaming everything on...

Chapter Two

War Stories

IMAGINE THIS. Picture in your mind you are sixteen and just received your driver's license. And to mark your special day you and a group of friends decide you want to visit the local mall. You all pile into your car and take off. You and your three African-American girlfriends are rocking to some music and enjoying each others' company. Of course you are obeying all the traffic rules because, after all, you just received your license and don't want it taken away. Besides, you've always been taught to be a law abiding citizen.

You've made it. You've arrived at your favorite store, Needless Markup. And just about the time you extract your keys from the ignition, three police squad cars appear, blaring red, flashing lights. As your right foot hits the heated pavement you are accosted by six Caucasian police officers who, at a hint of provocation, are ready to use their weapons. Since you watch the evening news and have seen what they are capable of doing, you decide to cooperate. After a quick glance at your girlfriends in the back seat who are trembling in fear, you call on the Lord for immediate protection.

About the time your blood pressure begins to return to normal, the security team from the mall arrives along with two more police officers and German shepherd dogs. Even though you have a strong willed personality, you know with one wrong move you are history. You take another deep breath and keep your cool.

By this time the officers are shouting at your three friends in the back seat to slowly exit the car. You fully cooperate even though four policemen are completing body searches on four teenage ladies. Audience gathers. One of the policemen gets the bright idea that he may have mistaken your identity.

Immediately your driver's license is thrown back at you and you are invited to resume your normal activities with not one hint of contrition from the policeman about your entire ordeal.

Does this appear to be racism? Please explain.

IMAGINE THIS. Think about preparing to depart for college in Wisconsin, as if moving away from home for the first time isn't traumatic enough. Before you leave, you use your gifts of administration and compile an exhaustive list of apartments available for rent. As you narrow the search, it seems logical to secure housing within walking distance of the University.

Before you pack your car, you call the owner of the apartment complex. A Caucasian-sounding woman answers and assures you that with two months security deposit and a signed lease you can have the apartment.

Hardly able to contain your excitement you head off to Wisconsin. When you arrive you introduce yourself, shake the woman's hand and suddenly you are faced with, "Oh! That apartment…I rented it yesterday."

Does this appear to be racism? Please explain.

IMAGINE THIS. An African-American woman approaches the checkout counter in a grocery store. The Caucasian cashier sizes her up by looking at her appearance and the type of groceries she has. When she opens her purse she is asked, "How are you planning to pay for your groceries, with money or food stamps?"

Does this appear to be racism? Please explain.

IMAGINE THIS. You're in the doctor's office. Present are a Caucasian nurse and an African-American man. You enter with two children and begin the intake process. The nurse intercepts your paperwork and, before examining the forms, assumes you are on governmental assistance and tells you, "Sorry, we are not taking any more public aid patients at this time."

Does this appear to be racism? Please explain.

IMAGINE THIS. You are an African-American woman in a major department store. Three Caucasian clerks look on. You are in quite a hurry and have no time for drama. But as you begin to shop, three Caucasian clerks follow you around the store watching your every move. Around the tenth time of them asking to help you and being followed by a plain-clothed security officer you leave in total frustration, unable to make your purchase.

Does this appear to be racism? Please explain.

IMAGINE THIS. You are an African-American male in the elevator of one of the tallest buildings in the United States. The door opens to reveal an elderly Caucasian woman. She is startled but is able to regain her composure. Just as she is about to enter the elevator she clutches her purse and suddenly remembers she forgot something in one of the offices.

Does this appear to be racism? Please explain.

IMAGINE THIS. You are an African-American boy of twelve standing before a bank teller of the Anglo Saxon persuasion. "Sir, this signature does not match the one on file. You'll have to sign this slip again. It still doesn't match. Try again. You know what, I'll have to talk with my supervisor." Enter the supervisor (of the same hue). "We need to see two forms of identification—a driver's license and a social security card." You respond, "I'm only twelve. I am not driving yet."

Does this appear to be racism? Please explain.

You might say that this all took place twenty years ago. "This is the twenty-first century. Racism doesn't exist anymore." Well let me tell you, racism is alive and quite well! Case in point. This book was completed in 2003. Just one year prior, an African-American woman with who I am very well acquainted tried to purchase a home in a west suburban neighborhood of Chicago. This woman, oblivious to housing discrimination in the twenty-first century, joyfully inspected all the homes while the owners were at home.

About the fifth time her contract was rejected, she realized, "Houston, I think we have a problem." Seeking guidance from the Lord, He revealed to her she need not visit the next homes. And since the realtor had been dragged through thirty homes, he certainly knew her taste.

One day while driving through the neighborhood she wanted to live in, she noticed a "for sale by owner" sign. Recalling previous experiences, she decided not to ring the doorbell. Instead she drove out of the driveway and called the owners on her cell phone. To her delight there were enough bedrooms and it was in her price range. Again relying on wisdom from God, she told the owner she would send a representative.

She called her realtor who was Caucasian, told him that if the home looked as immaculate as it did from the outside to make them an offer they could not refuse. The realtor, skilled in the art of negotiation, closed the deal without her ever inspecting the home. The only hurdle was the owners wanted to meet her in person. The realtor was able to convince them she was too busy.

In a few days the deal was closed, and she had a signed, sealed and delivered contract in her hands. You'll never guess what happened next. When an African-American home inspector showed up, the owners were quite startled! After refusing him entrance, the realtor called the buyer and informed her of their opposition to the home inspection.

She simply contacted their attorney and told him with great meekness that housing discrimination was against the law, and either they could sell her the home or she would be happy to receive it in a settlement in the largest housing discrimination suit in DuPage County history. About thirty years ago, another large litigation case involved an African-American business man who couldn't purchase a home in Oak Brook. Not only did he receive enough money from that settlement to purchase the home they wouldn't allow him to, but he could afford to buy the entire block.

After a quick consultation with my attorney, they figured they would rather sell me the home than give it to me.

In summation, why should African Americans have to make a major purchase such as a home without ever seeing it? What if I didn't like it after I placed a contract on it? Why should an African-American teenager be afraid to drive? Why should a college student be denied an apartment? Why should a security officer follow an African American around a department store as if they had stolen something? Why should an African-American man be humiliated by someone not willing to get on an elevator who is holding her purse tightly? Why can't an African-American mother shop for groceries without assumptions being made about her financial status? Why can't an African-American male buy a luxury sports car without someone assuming it is from drug money? How about a moratorium on policemen stopping all African Americans just for one day? Maybe we can have "We Won't Stop African Americans Today" as a national holiday in our honor to be annually commemorated.

Before we continue on with our quest to race towards reconciliation, I want to ask you to keep an open mind about our discussion. If you are not African American you probably think we are making a mole hill into a mountain. You are probably thinking there are other variables operating and that you need to hear the other side of the story to get all the facts. And of course there are always three sides of the story—your side, the individual you are in conflict with, and the Lord's. If you aren't willing to try on the shoes of your fellow man, you will never truly understand their plight. So I invite you to lay aside your judgments and frame of reference for the rest of this book. Take off your shoes and consider that these incidents could possibly be reality. Even if they aren't yours!

Our perception of individuals and their circumstances is half the battle in our race towards reconciliation. If we don't possess objectivity, we will have difficulty discerning the challenges and situations associated with race. Every one of us has our own perspective based on our experiences. Unfortunately this myopic view dictates how we will respond to one another. For instance, whenever I am thrust into a room with Caucasians I always detect I am being sized up. I strongly sense I am being judged from my physical appearance, the way I walk, my communication skills and my interaction among the people. It isn't until I begin conversing that I am able to dispel stereotypes associated with my race and gender. I cannot count the numerous occasions I've had Caucasian people tell me, "You are not like most black people," (as if we all fit into a neat little category).

So the next time you are tempted to judge someone based on their appearance, take a moment to ask the Lord to help you look at their heart instead.

Let's do a little perception experiment.

Perception Experiment 1

Directions: Enlist the help of two individuals in your small group who you don't know anything about. Allow the participants an opportunity to write down observations of subject A based on their physical appearance only. Subject B will be asked a series of questions (below). The goal of the experiment is to determine if your perception of Subject A and Subject B were accurate based on the appearance of Subject A and the questions answered by Subject B. **Describe Subject A's physical appearance. What conclusions can you draw from his/ her appearance about his/ her economic status, place of residence, occupation, marital status, how many children, mental health, age, and educational attainment.**

1. **Describe Subject B's physical appearance.**

2. **What is their emotional state like?** ***Are you happy today?***

3. **What is their economical status?** ***What city do you live in? What's the square footage of your home? How many bedrooms? What's your favorite hobby? Where do you go on vacation?***

4. **What do they do for a living?** ***Where did you attend college? Do you travel for your job? Do you work at a Fortune 500 company?***

5. **Are they married?** ***Do you have more married friends or single? Do you have children?***

6. **Are they Democratic or Republican?** ***Do you like our current president?***

7. **What is their religion?** ***Do you attend church?***

8. **What type of car do they drive? *What's your favorite car?***

9. **Do you have a summer home? *Where do you go in the summer?***

10. **What are their hobbies? *How do you spend your free time?***

11. **How much is their net worth? *How long have you been employed? Do you own more than one home?***

12. **How many times have they traveled to Europe? *Do you like Europe?***

13. **How old are they? *Are you considered a baby boomer?***

14. **What is their educational status? *How many educational loans did you have to pay back? How much were they?***

The objective of this experiment is to prove that in order to dispel myths and stereotypes about other individuals we need to spend an inordinate amount of time becoming acquainted with them. In the first case (with all variables being equal) we had absolutely no interaction with the individual and we had to assume characteristics about them that were totally inaccurate. For subject B we spent more time trying to know the individual, therefore we were able to make better judgments about them. In order to race towards reconciliation we will have to do the same thing. We hate what we can't relate to. So in order to appreciate that person we have to spend more time becoming acquainted with them. Many of our perceptions of individuals are based on their physical appearance. To validate this point I completed a little unscientific experiment of my own. (no letters please)

Perception Experiment 2

The next time you have a day off and want to experience how you are perceived by others, dress extremely casual and ride the train to a metropolitan area. Just observe how people treat you. I did my own such experiment. This is my data.

NARRATIVE: On January 7, 2003 I rode the train from a western suburb to Chicago. I was dressed as a homeless person, with a huge overcoat, holes in my tennis shoes and blue jeans, a baseball cap and torn gloves. When I tried to enter the train, four Caucasian men walked in front of me. The Caucasian woman right ahead of me allowed the door to slam in my face. As I began to search for a seat, an older Caucasian woman clutched her purse. A professional Caucasian man indicated with his body language the seat was unavailable to me. When I was about to sit down, an interracial couple literally moved out of disgust that I would sit next to them. A Hispanic man avoided eye contact with me when I smiled. A Caucasian woman decided she needed to make a cell phone call in order to avoid interaction with me. By the time I arrived in Chicago I'd received enough mistreatment that I desperately wanted to run into the nearest restroom and change my identity.

After I departed the train, I walked into the station. Every person I encountered refused eye contact. Again Caucasian men walked in front of me. An African-American man who was dressed similar to me smiled and said hello. Out of the twenty people I smiled at only two returned the smile. As soon as I entered the restroom, two elderly Caucasian women grabbed their purses which had been resting on the countertop. Three African-American women who stood in the line avoided interacting with me despite my several attempts to initiate a conversation with them. An Asian woman to whom I offered a paper towel to dry her hands refused it. When I asked the Caucasian police officer who was standing outside the door for directions, he suggested I read a map. Two Caucasian restaurant managers stood guard in front of their door and assigned their busboys to persuade me from panhandling. I hailed a cab. After twenty refusals I took the bus. When I approached the bus driver, he sized me up and asked me to pay before he pulled away from the curb. Wow! You would have thought I had leprosy.

On a positive note, before you give up on humanity, the ticket agent on board the train allowed me to ride for free, pretending as though he had already taken my ticket.

And before you offer the judgment that these observations are skewed, I followed the entire routine the following day except I was dressed professionally from head to toe. I wore a black business suit with a leather coat and boots along with my expensive jewelry. The results were totally different. I was greeted with smiles. Men allowed me to walk in front of them. The train door was held open for me. Three professional men with cell phones protruding from their ears sat and engaged in meaningful conversation with me. The ticket agent never asked for my money (I did pay him). When I walked into the train station, eighteen out of twenty commuters either smiled or acknowledged me. During my trip to the restroom, the women in line joked and dialogued with me about how cold it was. The policeman not only directed me to the taxi cab stand, he literally walked me to the door. The first hailed taxi responded. What a difference a day can make!

OBSERVATIONS: No particular racial group capitalizes on prejudice. Every group in the study had perceived me as being impoverished and treated me accordingly to their perception.

It's strictly human behavior to judge another individual's worth based on our perception of them. We bring to the table our own prejudices based on our own experiences and our childhood rearing. These prejudices, if they are not confined to a realistic view of our world, can develop into full-blown hatred.

Before I began my ministry working with homeless people, I asked the Lord to allow me to view them from the same perspective as He did. It radically changed my outlook on life. I could no longer stand in judgment of them if I was to minister to their physical, social, emotional and spiritual needs. Not only did I need to relate to them, but I needed to become one of them. Just as Jesus came to spend time with the afflicted, poor, and outcast, we must also strive to hang out with those who are different from us.

Chapter Three

Tolerance or Indifference

In the history of western civilization as we know it today, the one topic that stirs up more controversy than any other subject, with the exception of religion and politics, is the issue of race relations in America. Just a mere mention of words like multiculturalism, ethnicity, capital punishment, reparations or affirmative action can evoke heated debate and more sparks than an Independence Day fireworks display.

Why does the issue of race cause major world wars, nations to crumble and innocent blood shed? The Bible has only one answer to that. It's not a skin problem. It's a sin problem. From the day Adam and Eve disobeyed the Lord in the Garden of Eden, and through their seed, Cain and Able, they were responsible for nations being against nations.

Another significant contributor to racial tension was Sarai and her husband Abram who thought they needed to take matters into their own hands regarding their desire to be parents. According to Genesis chapter 16, "Now Sarai, Abram's wife, had borne him no children. But she had an Egyptian maidservant named Hagar; so she said to Abram, 'The Lord has kept me from having children. Go, sleep with my maidservant; perhaps I can build a family through her.' Abram agreed to what Sarai said. So after Abram had been living in Canaan ten years, Sarai his wife took her Egyptian maidservant Hagar and gave her to her husband to be his wife. He slept with Hagar, and she conceived. When she knew she was pregnant she began to despise her mistress. Then Sarai said to Abram, 'You are responsible for the wrong I am suffering. I put my servant in your arms, and now that she knows she is pregnant, she despises me. May the Lord judge between you and me.' 'Your servant is in your hands,' Abram said. 'Do with her whatever you think best.' Then Sarai mistreated Hagar; so she fled from her. The angel of the Lord found Hagar near a spring in the desert; it was the spring that is beside the road to Shur. And he said, 'Hagar, servant of Sarai, where have you come from, and where are you going?' 'I'm running away from my mistress Sarai,' she answered. Then the angel of the Lord told her, 'Go back to your mistress and submit to her.' The angel added, 'I will so increase your descendants that they will be too numerous to count.' The angel of the Lord also said to her: 'You are now with child and you will have a son. You shall name him Ishmael, for the Lord has heard of your misery. He will be a wild donkey of a man; his hand will be against everyone and everyone's hand against him, and he will live in hostility toward all his brothers.'"

So there you have it—the beginning of all this racial division. The first illustration of strife is in the opening pages of Genesis. And from that day on we have witnessed the effects of one nation against another nation.

Before we can cure the illness of racism we must first define all its symptoms. Race is defined by Webster's New World Dictionary as "any of the different varieties of mankind, mainly the Caucasoid, Mongoloid or Negroid groups distinguished by kind of hair, color of skin, stature, etc." Based on these characteristics the individual is expected to act a certain way and should also expect to be treated accordingly. Racism for this purpose is defined as prejudice based on race, influenced by power and resources of the dominant culture.

Racism can be an overt or covert operation. Some people are deliberate in their actions and some people are accessories after the fact. An example of overt racism is when an African-American individual inquires about an apartment rental via telephone, only to arrive in person and be told the unit is already rented. An example of covert racism is when that same individual tries to purchase a house and the Caucasian home owners decide she should put up $25,000 in earnest money for the property.

Racism can occur in the following systems: environmental, educational, religious, cultural, economical, legal, political and military. It occurs in three settings: individual, cultural and institutional. Racism as it relates on an individual basis was communicated when the woman in our earlier example got on the elevator and when an African American male wanted to share the same elevator she clutched her purse and immediately exited.

Cultural racism is characterized as acts of discrimination based on the notion that there is some type of genetic trait that determines intellectual qualities, socialization and morality of African Americans as inferior. Consequently, many people think they have a legitimate basis for their ill treatment of African Americans.

An example of this was during my senior year of high school my Caucasian guidance counselor told me I should explore a career in the military to finance my college education because I would never get into a college because of my low scores on entrance examination.

The final setting is institutional racism where practices, laws and access to material goods or resources are difficult to attain whether or not the intention was discrimination. An example would be the denial of an Ivy League education for an African American simply because it was not affordable.

Name the eight systems racism can be found in:

1.
2.
3.
4.
5.
6.
7.
8.

Give one example of racism from each system. (Example: Legal-racial profiling of African-American men.)

1.
2.
3.
4.
5.

6.
7.
8.

Name the three settings of racism.
1.
2.
3.

Give one example of each setting from your own experience or from someone else in your small group:
1.
2.
3.

In order to get at the heart of the problem we need to define additional terms.

Prejudice is defined by Webster's New World Dictionary as "an opinion formed before the facts are known: a preconceived idea, usually one that is unfavorable." Prejudice is not an innate quality. It is learned. I know preschool children who, if given an opportunity to play with African-American children, would favor that over playing with a child who is of the same culture. It's the parental and societal influence that shapes the child's perception of others. Even my daughter with special needs, although she doesn't have the capabilities of other children, still receives birthday invitations in our community. When we arrive the parents are sometimes quite surprised she's disabled because their children have never referred to her as such. Children usually don't judge the outward appearance unless they have been taught. They generally focus on matters of the heart. We adults should take notice of these qualities.

Prejudice is an equal opportunity destroyer. Everyone on earth has a prejudice about someone or something. My particular prejudices are against wealthy people. I don't care what complexion you are, if you are wealthy I don't particularly care for you. My prejudices are based on the way I perceive a few wealthy people, based on their behavior, and I've ascribed it to the entire group.

Is my prejudice sensible? Of course it isn't. Do you know why it isn't? It is not sensible because I have befriended people who are rich yet live in modest homes and do not have lavish life styles. In fact most of their money is donated to the church. So my prejudice is inaccurate now based on the definition above.

So why do we have prejudices when they conflict with the definition?

Name three prejudices you have about anything:
1.

2.

3.

What do you base these prejudices on?

Another term we must familiarize ourselves with is discrimination. It is defined by Webster's New World Dictionary as "a showing of partiality or prejudice in treatment; specific policies directed against the welfare of minority groups." This occurs when the majority holds back resources from minorities because of preconceived ideas about the group.

Example: College scholarships are inaccessible to African-American students because the majority who are responsible for allocating the funds may feel they are educationally inferior, which may be a valid hypothesis. Okay. Let's say that the average IQ scores of African-American children are below average. That may be true. But there are an inordinate amount of variables confirming this. Many African-American children comprise our inner-city schools.

We all know in the inner city there is extreme poverty. We are aware that the schools are funded by property taxes. Since the median priced home in the poverty stricken area is significantly lower than the property taxes in suburban areas, the money that would be designated for the school district in an inner city would be quite minimal. Less money translates into fewer educational resources and less qualified staff for these African-American children. The consequences: lower test scores. In fact, I have friends who teach in the Chicago Public School system who complain about the lack of financial resources that renders them helpless in their attempts to educate. They comment on how they are often forced to pass the children on to the next grade level. This creates an even wider chasm because now you have children not able to grasp educational concepts yet are continuously promoted to the next grade.

In that example we tapped into three different affects. Racism occurs when college scholarships are inaccessible. Prejudice occurs when college administrators set their standard for testing to accommodate mainstream society. And discrimination occurs when these same students are denied entrance. Sometimes these effects are interchangeable and sometimes they function independently of each other.

Oftentimes discrimination operates because the dominant culture doesn't want to be inconvenienced. For example, it took legislation for the school system to recognize special needs children. The litigation on behalf of the children addressed the need for schools to accommodate these precious children. Who knows what type of educational resources my daughter with cerebral palsy would have had in the early 1970s if she had been in school at the time without the court system's intervention? Not like it's a piece of cake now. But at least we have a host of legal rights we can explore if necessary.

The same with the Hispanic population (who have, incidentally, surpassed African Americans in population). How inconvenient it would be if mainstream society had to suddenly teach these individuals English and have Spanish translators in the interim, as well as print signs and instructions in their native language. What if we have to start recognizing Cinco De Mayo as a national holiday? What about Hispanic political candidates? Wow! What a challenge! What about the accommodations we will have to make for them in the upcoming years? I really don't think it's worth it. (That is the malignant mentality of the majority.)

In any attempt to reconcile cross-culturally, we must recognize that we are all unique and bring to the melting pot a spicy stew. "If all of us were alike some of us would be unnecessary."

Stereotype is another term we need to define. It is defined by Webster's New World Dictionary as "a fixed idea or popular conception about how a certain type of person looks, acts, etc." My definition of the word is, "Stereotypes are an unrealistic prejudgment of a group of people based on their culture, class, economic status or gender and are perceived in a certain way because of negative images from mainstream society."

Name four negative images associated with African Americans you have observed in the last month through the media.

1.

2.

3.

4.

Why are these stereotypes negative?

Are stereotypes always negative?

What types of behaviors do they reinforce?

The stereotypes you have listed above are no more reality than the stereotypes I held about Italian men for several years. In order to race towards reconciliation we will need to dispel any stereotypes we seek to ascribe to any culture. To accomplish this will take some reconditioning and renewing of the mind. Next time you are tempted to categorize a group of people try this exercise: (Unscientific—no letters please!)

Stereotype: All Italian men are associated with the Mafia.

Exercise: Ask twenty-five Italian men what their occupations are.

Stereotype: Women with natural blonde hair are unintelligent.

Exercise: Survey fifteen natural-blonde-haired women and ask what their grade point average was in high school or college. Survey fifteen black-haired women and ask their grade point average in high school or college. Average each set of scores to determine which group scored higher.

In order to attain a perspective of your own philosophy of race relations, we need to begin with the biblical perspective of racial diversity. According to Acts 17:26, "From one man he made every nation of men, that they should inhabit the whole earth; and he determined the times set for them and the exact places they should live." Some individuals have surmised from this verse that we were all destined to live separately. This Scripture doesn't imply that at all. It merely communicates that we are all from one man, and from him all nationalities and races were born. We are all from the same blood type—literally and figuratively. We are part of a universal family with the same Daddy. No nation or race can have a monopoly on God's favor. He has no illegitimate children.

The Bible refers to the word race as being the origin or unity of all humanity. According to that passage we are all members of the human race. This membership we have in common means we all have our ancestry in Adam and Eve. And like our first parents we all are sinners who will die, and have a need for Jesus Christ in our lives.

There are absolutely no references in the Bible that speak negatively about any groups of people. The only time there was a distinction made of a group was when they disobeyed God. The Bible only condemns the Philistines, Gentiles, Samaritans and Canaanites based on their inability to worship the true and living God. It does not denounce them because of their nationality. As soon as they began to accept God's teaching the negative stigmas were removed.

As Christ followers we are required to adopt the biblical view of race. In order to achieve this we will have to reprogram our minds. Just like a computer, whatever data you enter, that will be the data you retrieve. If you grew up in a family that acknowledged negative differences in cultures you are going to have a more difficult time changing your program. The difference is you can draw on the Holy Spirit's power to effect change. On the other hand, if you grew up in a family where there was indifference to race relations you will have to change your data into a more proactive program. You will have to make it a point to seek out reconciliation by initiating opportunities. As a Christ follower you simply can no longer be contented with the status quo.

Early Childhood Experiences Worksheet

In order to begin our race towards reconciliation, you need to record your thoughts about your early childhood experiences of how your parents and extended family members dealt with the issues of race.

At what age were you first exposed to a member of a different race? Please explain.

What was your perception of your parents' views regarding the individual? Please explain.

Was this view right or wrong? Please explain.

Did you parents aggressively pursue friendships with members of different cultures? Please explain.

Did your parents ever speak negatively concerning another race? Please explain.

Did it ever influence your thinking? Please explain.

Did you perceive your parents as being prejudiced? Please explain.

Did they ever offer excuses when you wanted to interact with someone of a different culture? Please explain.

How did your peers respond to people of a different culture in your school setting? Please explain.

If your friends made derogatory remarks about a racial group, how did you usually respond? Please explain.

During your childhood, did you ever witness discrimination either from your own experience or from someone else's? Please explain.

Recall any immoral actions your parents communicated to you during your childhood that you terminated when you became an adult. Please explain.

How were you able to avert them? Please explain.

Do you feel racial reconciliation can be achieved through the same techniques you used for overcoming immoral actions? Please explain.

Write down four lies the devil has told you concerning African Americans. Record under your response what God's Word says about African Americans.

Example:

1. **I was told that African Americans were immoral drug addicts who lack motivation.**
2. **"All have sinned and fallen short of the glory of God."**

1.
2.

1.
2.

1.
2.

1.
2.

Prejudice, as stated previously, is a learned behavior. Children do not innately hate unless they have role models who teach them through words or deeds. For instance, I completed an unscientific study to measure prejudice in children (this was an amateurish analysis; please no letters from psychologists). I selected twenty-five children ages three to six. The goal was to determine whether preschool children recognized skin color. I gave them a choice of multicultural modeling clay—the colors were tan, brown, beige, terra-cotta, sienna, and cream. I asked them to mold the clay into the shape of a person they admire.

The results: one three-year-old made the person they most admired using the tan, one three-year-old used the sienna color, five four-year-olds used the brown color, ten five-year-olds used the terra-cotta color, six six-year-olds used the beige color, only one four-year-old used cream, and one three-year-old used cream that he mixed with the brown color. (Perhaps he was living in a multiracial household.)

Each child had equal access to all of the colors. The cream color was the closest color to white. There were absolutely no teachers allowed in the experiment area and there was no coaching of any type. When I asked who some of the people they admired were, twenty of the children answered their parents, which was quite surprising to me seeing as how eighteen of the children surveyed were Caucasian. It was also interesting to observe that the one Asian child, one African-American children, one Pakistani child, one Hispanic child, and one multiracial child all used the brown color. I can't help but speculate as to what the variables would be if we polled children of school age. The six-year-olds in the study had not yet started kindergarten. Perhaps by the time they arrive at school their perceptions of color might be different. I will track the six-year-old children next year after they have attended at least four months of school to evaluate whether the results will be the same.

Tolerance is derived from the word tolerate and is defined by Webster's New World Dictionary as "to recognize and respect other's beliefs, practices etc. without sharing them. As Christ followers this definition is not acceptable if we are one with the same Daddy Jesus. For me to recognize you as a Caucasian and not celebrate St. Patrick's Day, Columbus Day, or any ethnic holiday has a tendency to alienate us. To not acknowledge our Jewish brother's and sisters at Passover or Hanukkah could probably communicate to them that we will recognize your belief but just don't ask us to share in your celebration. Why not? What is wrong with seeking out a celebration of a Seder dinner where you and your entire family can participate. Our family serves corn beef, potatoes and sauerkraut on St. Patrick's Day. On Cinco De Mayo we have a Mexican meal.

How many members of your immediate family when they are celebrating a birthday, graduation or anniversary you have the attitude I respect that you are turning another year older or you are graduating from college, or you've celebrated another year of marriage however, don't expect me to share in your happiness after all I don't agree with your politics or your religious ideologies.

The other spectrum of tolerance is indifference. Indifference defined for this purpose means "a lack of concern because it is not important." Apathy is the sister to this term. I have people who approach me in the community who fervently feel they have to defend themselves regarding their lack of motivation for reconciling cross-culturally. They greet me with, "I am not prejudiced. I like black people. I've never discriminated against anyone. I don't speak ill of them." But when I ask them how many black friends they have, and when was the last time they socialized with a group of African Americans, they suddenly want to change the subject. Just because you don't speak ill of a group and you generally like them doesn't mean you are reconciled. No more than it means that you are a car because you've been in the garage.

If you are apathetic in relating cross-culturally you are really no different than an individual who is tolerant. For example, if your daughter was engaged and you did absolutely nothing to get more acquainted with your future son-in-law, how do you think they would both feel? They would probably think you didn't want him in their family. Or they could possibly think that you don't have your daughter's best interest at heart. Or they could also think that you are quite selfish and preoccupied with your own self-interest that you have no time for anyone else.

The same with reconciling cross-culturally if you don't proactively seek out relationships with African Americans we might think you don't want us in your family. Remember what Acts 17:26 states, "From one man he made every nation." So to disavow any recognition of African Americans as part of your family is a sin. If you are not reconciling with us we might feel you don't have our best interest at heart. If we cannot trust you how will we ever be able to be in relationship with you? We've seen countless examples in our community of how one spouse may have committed adultery and how it takes several years for the offended spouse to be able to trust again. Once that trust is destroyed it is hard to maintain a covenant relationship. If we are to trust you we first need to make sure you are clearly committed to your goals.

In order for reconciliation to be effective we also need to make sure you are not motivated by guilt or your own self-interest. I know businessmen who enjoy the tax benefits they receive when they hire African Americans. But if you ask them how many of their African-American employees are Chief Executive Officers, or sit on the board of directors, they will respond with a blank stare on their faces. Are you motivated out of a sense of duty, because it's the white thing to do? Or do you feel sorry for African Americans? If you are not motivated by the biblical mandate of Mark 12:31 "Love your neighbor as yourself" then perhaps you need to wallow in your passiveness and champion another cause.

Chapter Four

A Biblical Perspective

Before we can reconcile with our brothers and sisters cross-culturally, we must first be reconciled to Jesus Christ. According to 2 Corinthians 5:18-21, "All this is from God, who reconciled us to himself through Christ and gave us the ministry of reconciliation: that God was reconciling the world to himself in Christ, not counting men's sins against them. And he has committed to us the message of reconciliation. We are therefore Christ's ambassadors, as though God were making his appeal through us. We implore you on Christ's behalf: Be reconciled to God. God made him who had no sin to be sin for us, so that in him we might become the righteousness of God."

God takes the initiative to redeem us. He sustains us and brings redemption to completion in our lives. We who receive His reconciliation are new creations and vessels of God to minister this message throughout the world. When Christ endured the punishment of sin that should have been ours, He made it possible for us to be reconciled to God. This redemption is freely offered and all who ask shall receive.

If you are serious about racing towards reconciliation and you have never accepted Christ as your personal Savior becoming reconciled to Jesus is very easy. Are you ready to take that step? If you said yes, all you have to do is believe what Romans 10:9 states, "That if you confess with your mouth, 'Jesus is Lord,' and believe in your heart that God raised him from the dead, you will be saved."

See how easy this is? All you have to do is confess, believe and receive. If you did those three things, **WELCOME TO THE KINGDOM OF GOD!** You are officially a born-again Christian. All you have to do next is attend a local Bible-teaching church and they will assist you with the rest of your growth. Please feel free to contact me for more information and reading resources to assist you with growing in your new faith.

If you decided not to accept Christ at this time you can still read on, but the strategies for reconciling won't be as effective for you as a nonbeliever. Only those of us who belong to Jesus will have an easier time reconciling, because of the power of the Holy Spirit that richly dwells within us.

If you are utilizing this resource as an educational tool in a secular setting, the way to maximize its effectiveness is to at least secure the services of a facilitator who is a Christ follower.

Any attempt at reconciling cross-culturally is like placing a lion in a cage with a cat. Although they are from the same species they have vast differences. The same could be said about a couple after the honeymoon is over. Any time you bring two groups of people together from different backgrounds who have been separated by a system of oppression, mistreatment, mistrust, and suspicion and try to sit at a table to sign a peace treaty it won't be easy.

The only way to begin this race is to attach it to spiritual reconciliation. It has to be viewed in the context of ministry and pursued feverishly. The mature follower of Christ should allow the Word of God and the life example of Jesus to pattern their behavior. We have to love others at all costs. This involves the actual laying down our life for a friend. We are to adopt Colossians 3:8-14 which states, "But now you must rid yourselves of all such things as these: anger, rage, malice, slander and filthy language from your lips. Do not lie to each other, since you have taken off your old self with its practices and have put on the new self, which is being renewed in knowledge in the image of its Creator. Here there is no Greek or Jew, circumcised or uncircumcised, barbarian, Scythian, slave or free, but Christ is all, and is in all. Therefore, as God's chosen people, holy and dearly loved, clothe yourselves with compassion, kindness, humility, gentleness and patience. Bear with each other and forgive whatever grievances you may have against one another. Forgive as the Lord forgave you. And over all these virtues put on love, which binds them all together in perfect unity."

The key words here are new self and chosen people. This means once we accept Jesus as our Savior we become a new man (or woman) and we become His regardless of our race. As His chosen ones we are holy and have the Holy Spirit guiding us in all areas of our lives. This Scripture also suggests that in order to be effective in racial reconciliation we have to wear love and walk in complete forgiveness.

As Christ followers we are called to live out a different standard in our world. To reject this reality means we are rejecting the very teachings of God. The first example of reconciling occurred before Jesus Christ was even born. This is evidenced in His genealogy, in Matthew 1:1-16.

List the Gentiles in Jesus's genealogy.

1.
2.
3.
4.
5.

Since Jesus was Jewish, His having Gentiles in His lineage signified that God had a heart for reconciliation. Before the birth of Jesus we can already see that was the Lord's idea.

Another important example of God's heart for reconciliation occurred when the Magi visited the baby Jesus. These men represented various nations. Their mere presence communicated that God had called all nations to enjoy a sweet communion with His Son, Jesus. Yet another example was the pronouncement of Simeon in Luke 2:29-32, "'Sovereign Lord, as you have promised, you now dismiss your servant in peace. For my eyes have seen your salvation, which you have prepared in the sight of all people, a light for revelation to the Gentiles and for glory to your people Israel.'"

Later in His ministry in Mark 5:1-20 we find Jesus entered into the region Gerasenes, a territory inhabited by Gentiles. In Matthew 15:21-28, a Canaanite woman begged Jesus to heal her demon-possessed daughter. Jesus responded by saying He was only sent to the lost sheep of Israel and it was not right to take the children's bread and toss it to their dogs. She responded by saying that she knew, but even the dogs eat the crumbs that fall from their master's table.

In Luke 7:1-10, He comes to the rescue of a Roman centurion's servant. Not only was Jesus interested in reconciling cross-culturally but also in the class system. He responded to a man who was in authority and merely said a word to heal the man's servant.

My all-time favorite story of reconciliation is the encounter He had with the Samaritan woman at the well. Let's take a closer look.

According to John 4:4-30, "Now he had to go through Samaria. So he came to a town in Samaria called Sychar, near the plot of ground Jacob had given to his son Joseph. Jacob's well was there, and Jesus, tired as he was from the journey, sat down by the well. It was about the sixth hour. When a Samaritan woman came to draw water, Jesus said to her, 'Will you give me a drink?' (His disciples had gone into the town to buy food.) The Samaritan woman said to him, 'You are a Jew and I am a Samaritan woman. How can you ask me for a drink?' (For Jews do not associate with Samaritans.) Jesus answered her, 'If you knew the gift of God and who it is that asks you for a drink, you would have asked him and he would have given you living water.' 'Sir,' the woman said, 'you have nothing to draw with and the well is deep. Where can you get this living water? Are you greater than our father Jacob, who gave us the well and drank from it himself, as did also his sons and his flocks and herds?' Jesus answered, 'Everyone who drinks this water will be thirsty again, but whoever drinks the water I give him will never thirst. Indeed, the water I give him will become in him a spring of water welling up to eternal life.' The woman said to him, 'Sir, give me this water so that I won't get thirsty and have to keep coming here to draw water.' He told her, 'Go, call your husband and come back.' 'I have no husband,' she replied. Jesus said to her, 'You are right when you say you have no husband. The fact is, you have had five husbands, and the man you now have is not your husband. What you have just said is quite true.' 'Sir,' the woman said, 'I can see that you are a prophet. Our fathers worshipped on this mountain, but you Jews claim that the place where we must worship is in Jerusalem.' Jesus declared, 'Believe me, woman, a time is coming when you will worship the Father neither on this mountain nor in Jerusalem. You Samaritans worship what you do not know; we worship what we do know, for salvation is from the Jews. Yet a time is coming and has now come when the true worshipers will worship the Father in spirit and truth, for they are the kind of worshipers the Father seeks. God is spirit and his worshipers must worship in spirit and in truth.' The woman said, 'I know that Messiah' (called Christ) 'is coming. When he comes, he will explain everything to us.' Then Jesus declared, 'I who speak to you am he.' Just then his disciples returned and were surprised to find him talking with a woman. But no one asked, 'What do you want?' or 'Why are you talking with her?' Then, leaving her water jar, the woman went back to the town and said to the people, 'Come, see a man who told me everything I ever did. Could this be the Christ?' They came out of the town and made their way toward him."

What a story! In verse 4 we see the first step Jesus made was very intentional. Just the mere fact He traveled through Samaria indicated He was on a serious mission. The Jews despised the Samaritans. There was intense hatred among the two groups. There was a schism between them that was longer than the wailing wall in Israel. The traditions of Jews at that time forbade any travel through that region. In fact earlier Jesus had advised His disciples not to enter any cities inhabited by the Samaritans. He didn't perform any miracles there nor preach publicly. His focus was on the lost sheep of Israel. So when He entered Samaria to reconcile, He was highly motivated. He gave up His personal safety and risked being ostracized by His fellow Jews, not to mention the possible rejection He could face by speaking to this woman.

Jesus went to her with great boldness and courage. He was willing to step out of His comfort zone. He went into her community. In doing this He communicated that He wanted to make her feel sheltered. He showed her that He cared enough to see that her security needs were being addressed. Furthermore, her name not mentioned in the Bible indicates the Lord's desire to protect her from any embarrassment.

In reconciling you have to go into our community. You have to take the initiative to eat our food, familiarize yourself with our music, customs and our traditions. This can only be accomplished in the context of interacting with us as opposed to being a tourist.

In verse 7 Jesus asked for a drink. He placed Himself in a very vulnerable position by asking for a drink from someone who was considered to be inferior to Him. He gave her the upper hand by asking her for help. He humbled Himself in her sight for the greater good, while at the same time identifying with her poverty. She recognized His humility because no Jew would ever ask a Samaritan for anything. She expected Jesus to be like the other Jews. She had her own preconceived ideas about Him and anticipated He would respond accordingly.

Many times our well-meaning Caucasian friends have a tendency to want to rush into a situation with a save-the-world mentality. Because you have political and economical resources you are able to come to our aid. In reconciliation it takes wisdom and discernment to figure out the best approach when wanting to assist us. When you run into our communities and drop off food it sometimes feels like you're patronizing us, especially when you don't invite us to participate in your planning. How about the next time you want to do a community project in our neighborhood, you invite the recipients to participate in the planning stages? We need to be empowered if we are going to reconcile. When you have the next board meeting, how about allowing an African-American individual on your staff to chair the meeting? When you are having a brain storming session, ask for their ideas concerning your project. Try to refrain from the-what-we-can-do-for-you mentality and focus on what we all can bring to the table.

In verse 8 we see that the disciples were on a different mission than Jesus was. Sometimes in order to reconcile cross-culturally you may have to leave your family members and friends behind. *Not everyone will share your same vision. It's better to carry out the Lord's mission in obedience by yourself or with those who do share your vision.*

In verse 9 the woman immediately recognized Jesus was a Jew and was quick to inform Jesus of the prejudices associated with their differences. Because we don't live in a color-blind society it's okay to recognize our differences. It's only when these differences alienate us that we get into trouble. We need to celebrate our uniqueness. The Samaritan woman made judgments based on His outward appearance. How many times have we done the same? We are all guilty. Recently I was mistaken for the homeless people I was intending to serve, based on my casual appearance.

In verse 10 we see that Jesus ignored the comment of who He was. She may have also been evading the issue because if she knew who He really was she would be forced to change. Since she had been married five times and was currently living in sin, she knew that once she made a commitment to Jesus she would have to repent.

Jesus was very gentle with her because He knew His approach was a matter of life or death and that it was simply not worth losing her soul, it should be the same with racial reconciliation. Strictly avoid any heated debates about prejudice or the sins of others. Satan revels when we make distinctions in our brothers and sisters, not only because it distracts us from the healing process, but also because it's an affront to our Creator who has fearfully and wonderfully made every one of us. We also see that Jesus treated her with respect. He stressed to her she was on equal footing with Him. He was very patient, gentle and compassionate with her. He did not set a tone that indicated He was superior to her. He just stated the facts. He met her where she was in her faith. Not only did He cross racial lines, He crossed gender lines.

In verse 11 we see that this woman was totally oblivious to who Jesus was. She just didn't get it. If she had only known this beggar could offer her a life-altering gift she would have taken it. She was operating in the natural. Her spiritual eyes were tightly closed. She didn't believe in Him because she had no tangible evidence.

In reconciling there will be individuals who won't believe that living peaceably with all men is possible because they are walking in the natural. Living peaceably is only possible through the power of the Holy Spirit. The natural water the woman was consumed with drinking would only quench her present thirst. But the living water Jesus could give her would yield lasting satisfaction.

Her motivation was based on a physical level. She was trying to satisfy her flesh. If your motivation for reconciling is based on a guilty conscience, you will be continuously thirsty. If you are truly motivated because of what Christ did on the cross and you see God's redemptive work on your behalf, you will have a long-lasting and satisfying journey on the narrow road to reconciliation. The water Christ gives is a spring of water that is pure, clear and flows freely. It never stagnates. It is symbolic of our spiritual life which should always be springing towards perfection. This desire to aim higher and press towards the mark should provide us with a thirst for reconciliation we cannot quench. We should be so fervent and passionate about our calling that we are flooded with opportunities to cross the bridge to racial reconciliation.

Sometimes in reconciling we have a tendency to judge the outward appearance of an individual. We fail to see they are a precious gift to us. We usually see what our role in their lives could be and how we may bless them, when in fact we ought to be the recipients of the blessing they are in our lives. Surely this woman thought she had the upper hand because Jesus needed something from her. She perceived Him as a poor and weary traveler. Jesus could have lorded His position over her because of who He was. But since her soul was at stake He tried a different approach.

In our quest to reconcile, you don't have to lord over us your skills, intellectual prowess, creativity and economical stability. God is no respecter of persons. What He's done for you He will do the same for us. In fact, to take credit for the gifts the Lord has given you is arrogance. And you know how He feels about pride.

When seeking relationships with African Americans, begin with a subject that makes us all equal, try to focus your conversations on our relationships with the Lord. Oftentimes in your haste to relate to us, you lack discretion by trying to compare yourself materially with what we've accumulated. Discussing what you do for a living if you are a neurologist and I am a janitor just sets us up for more alienation. Try to confine conversations to religion. When all else fails you can talk about the weather, sports or, one of my favorite topics, politics.

This woman was also so pragmatic and obsessed with propriety that she almost missed the entire point. Because she focused on the obvious she was concerned with appearances and tried to redirect the conversation. She tried to change the subject by telling Jesus He didn't have anything to draw with from the well. He assured her that living water translated to mean the Holy Spirit, and it was available to her for the asking, this is the same with reconciliation. If you ask the Lord to assist you with loving your brother cross-culturally, I guarantee you He will. I just caution you to be very careful of what you pray for. You will be setting yourself up to go places few men have gone before. Your comfort zone may be stretched when you ask the Lord to complete a good work in you. I double dare you to ask Him.

In verse 12 she asked Him if He was greater than Jacob. He certainly had the right to say yes because it was the truth. The truth of the matter is not what is always important in reconciling. The majority in this country have educational, economical, political and legal empowerment and access strictly attributed to their physical appearances. However, it doesn't necessarily need to be reinforced over and over again. For example, there is nothing wrong with affirmative action. I strongly believe African Americans should receive employment opportunities and college scholarships based on their racial identity, provided they are just as or more qualified than their Caucasian counterpart. The difference is the African-American student may have less accessibility to financial resources in his community, therefore he needs programs that will assist him. And until we find another viable solution we have to accept already existing programs and modify appropriately.

In verse 13 Jesus gave her another opportunity to respond to Him. He didn't belittle her by telling her she wasn't getting it. He simply restated His previous offer. In reconciling you may have to take several different approaches. No one approach is the best. You will have to try and try again until you find a strategy that works, and if you are rejected at your attempts don't take it personally. Perhaps that individual isn't ready to reconcile or had other issues. In that case shake the dust off your feet and take your message of hope to the next person. Or there's the opposite extreme where you are suddenly elevated to deity status because of your perseverance. Be very careful of those who seek to place you on a pedestal. Remember they spoke highly of the false prophets.

In verse 14 He made her an offer she could not refuse. In verse 15 she still hadn't realized the full revelation of who Jesus was. She had absolutely no clue what she was asking for. In reconciling we'd better ensure that when we ask the Lord to intercede on our behalf we are aware of the ramifications. If you are praying for the Lord to use you as a vessel for reconciliation you should be serious. You are setting yourself up for spiritual warfare. You may be persecuted, tried, tested, rebuked, scorned, exiled, ex-communicated and possibly held for ransom. Are you ready for all of that? Are you willing to possibly lay your life down for the cause?

In verse 16 He told her to go get her husband. Jesus made His intentions honorable and very clear by communicating to her the importance of getting her husband. He didn't leave any room for her to assume anything else. He showed her that He was also interested in her husband's redemption. In attempts at reconciliation, all parties involved and their spouses should always be invited to participate. This is a group effort. When interacting cross-culturally with the opposite sex and your spouse is absent, that's not reconciliation. That's called adultery! Bring your spouse to "avoid every kind of evil" (1 Thessalonians 5:2).

In verse 17 she told Him she didn't have a husband (as if He didn't know). One of the amazing observations from this was how Jesus allowed her to refer to her own sin. Jesus never condemns any of us. He allows the Holy Spirit to convict us. He allowed her to tell the truth about her own situation.

In order to reconcile you have to possess the ability to hear the truth about yourself. There will be some attributes about you that you may not want to address. But if we are destined to break down the barriers that surround our groups, you will at some point have to be open to hearing the truth, and not only hear the truth but be able to speak the truth in love. For example, if a group of African Americans are conversing and perceive that Caucasians are a certain way, even if you don't agree with it, because it is their reality we need to understand their perspective. As human beings we need to respect everyone's opinions even if it differs from ours. There may also be a time when you will have to make decisions concerning cross-cultural relationships which may not be popular. Or a time when someone may be speaking derogatorily of another race and you will be required to speak up.

In verses 17 and 18 we also see Jesus read her mind. At this point in reconciliation He earned the right to get into her business. Since He had invested time with her, treated her with respect, didn't treat her condescendingly and was concerned for her well being He had the authority to confront her. He made her feel like she was special. He didn't have to embarrass her. He knew that sometime during the conversation she would begin to recognize her own sin.

I would caution you that when you seek to be reconciled to your brother or sister in Christ you refrain from pointing out their sins. Many relationships are tainted because someone thought they had the blood-bought right to tell someone else how to live. Jesus is the only one who can tell us anything. For example, I befriended a young single mother who became a very good friend of the family. About six weeks into the relationship she started telling me how to raise my children. Keep in mind she was twenty years younger than I and had only one child at the time to the five I have. I realized that the conflict was mine and I admitted to her that I should have defined our relationship. She thought because I treated her as a family member that she had rights and privileges as any other member. It wasn't until I redefined our relationship that she had clear guidelines about how she should relate to me. I am happy to report that we were able to restore our friendship because of our open communication.

In verse 18 the Lord gave her the facts again and commended her for telling the truth. Just like when we have sinned and fallen short He takes one of our good qualities and focuses on that one instead of the others. In reconciling please try to focus on the positive traits of the individual instead of the negative. I learned this lesson from the teachers at my children's school. When they would call, they would always preface the conversation by saying my little Jonah (name changed) had a good day sharing toys with his friends. But in the afternoon he was fighting. I am amazed at how effective that technique is. Because she complimented me on how he had been previously, it literally deflected the negative. In reconciling, although this individual may have a political agenda and seems very militant concerning his or her race, try focusing on their positive attributes. Maybe they have other gifts. Try to bond with them on that level.

In verse 19 she immediately recognized Jesus was a prophet, evidenced by her referring to Him as sir. All of a sudden she had respect for Him. Any time someone can tell your life story and treat you with compassion you have to know they are sent from God. Of course there are some false prophets out there. But we have to be fruit inspectors. Does their life line up with God's Word? She knew He was a prophet simply because of the way He approached her.

We need to communicate to those we are trying to reconcile with that we are sent by God. We have to ensure them that this is a mandate from Him before we can expect them to trust us. Even when you are attempting to reconcile to the unsaved, when you mention the Lord is responsible for your changed heart, they will oftentimes not be wary of your intentions. I remember vividly when our youth group would wash people's cars for free. People couldn't believe it. They would always ask what the catch was, because nothing in life is free. When we told them it was because of the love we have for Jesus and for them, they would concede. We would end up with more donations by the close of the day simply because they knew what our motivations were.

In verse 20 she attempted a diversionary question. Since she was aware of Jesus's special insight she tried to get the inside track on a problem that had plagued her people for years. She wanted to know whether she was worshipping in the correct place. Whenever you are trying to reconcile, stay close to the subject. Define what your objective is and stay on task.

There was one case where a single Caucasian male friend of mine attempted to reconcile with a single African-American woman. His intentions were pure and true. He had no other motives. The short of it was she mistook his intentions for romance and they were both scorned. It took extensive counseling to heal those wounds. I am happy to report they have been happily married for twenty years. I guess you can say they reconciled very well! Please don't misunderstand me, there was nothing wrong with them marrying. The point I am trying to make is he needed to initially communicate his intentions towards her. He should have been honest and said, "It would be an honor in my attempts to racially reconcile if you would allow me to be your friend." This clear communication would have allowed her to be responsible for placing her emotions in check since the relationship had been defined. Later on if they became romantically inclined it was again his responsibility to say, "You know, I think this friendship is becoming more of a relationship. How do you feel about me? What is God telling you about our relationship? Do you see marriage as a possibility?" Communication is a key ingredient to reconciliation.

While attempting to reconcile don't allow anyone to change the subject. For over two hundred years we've been changing the subject regarding racism. Stand your ground! Whenever you become intimidated, annoyed, angry, or uncomfortable about the subject, you are headed in the right direction. The healing process can only occur when both parties lay down their pride and have vulnerability and a willingness to serve one another. Just like a marriage, both parties have to give 100 percent.

In verse 21 we clearly see Jesus's heart. He could have rebuked her and admonished her. Instead He gently guided her back to the truth by declaring that salvation is from the Jews. Let's not misinterpret this Scripture to mean that they are privileged people and no one else is entitled to salvation. All it is saying is that since Jesus was Jewish, that is where the salvation came from. He clarified it in verse 23 and 24 when He said that "the true worshippers will worship the Father in spirit and truth."

Jesus, when attempting to reconcile, didn't continue with a full theological explanation. He didn't offer her a lot of extra information. How many of us know that if you went up to a group of African-American people on the west side of Chicago and announced that you were there to reconcile with them that you would be laughed at and completely ostracized by the entire community? That isn't quite the approach we are looking for. The correct approach is to first of all divide and conquer. Never approach a group of people, because you have an audience. You are setting yourself up for a huge fall. Approach someone alone and on their own turf when possible like Jesus did or, if that isn't accessible, a neutral location such as the workplace, church, a restaurant, or a health club.

If you are an introvert, perhaps you can get friends or your small group together and ask the individual to join you. I know you are probably thinking about safety. We are aware of that. So since you are a Christ follower, ask the Holy Spirit for wisdom, discernment and protection. You could also seek counsel from your friends. And if all else fails, ask your spouse! He or she will know.

In verse 25, girlfriend was still quite oblivious to the divine appointment. She was clueless of who Jesus was. She tried to evade the issue. In reconciling keep trying even if it takes a hundred times. Try and try again. Continue on your journey until you receive your breakthrough. Remember how patient the Lord was with you and I before we came to Him? Keep that in mind when it seems like the individual still isn't clued in. People often want to hear from Jesus before they believe anything. So afford them that opportunity. If they are not quite ready to take the plunge give them their space. Allow the Holy Spirit to do a mighty work in their lives. He's the only one who can.

In verse 26 Jesus finally declared who He was. He tried desperately for her to arrive at the conclusion on her own. He reminded her that although she was of a different gender and religion, the core of her existence could be the Spirit if she would submit long enough. He was trying to communicate to her that although she was different, that the same Spirit He had could dwell within her.

In attempting to reconcile try not to alienate the individual by revealing your abilities. If you are in Christ, you are the most talented, beautiful, wise, wealthy, holy, righteous, resourceful, anointed, Holy Spirit-filled human being to have ever walked the face of the earth. You are operating with special gifts. You are wonderful! However, we are not to look at ourselves more highly than we ought to. *Point the way to the cross, not to yourself!* Be as vulnerable as possible. Let your guard down. At times you may have to literally take an individual by the hand and state who you are and why you are there. Use good judgment in all instances.

In verse 27 the disciples returned and were surprised Jesus was speaking with her. They were an interruption. Right as the breakthrough was peeking through the clouds, the disciples appeared from out of nowhere. In reconciling, expect some interruptions. I remember when I was about to discuss strategies for racial reconciliation with a leader at my church. The morning of the meeting my son was violently ill, I spilled chlorine bleach on a new pair of shoes, and to top it off I almost crashed into someone's car before I arrived at the meeting. The devil had another agenda for me that day. But the Lord prevailed because I was determined that "no weapon forged against [me] would prevail and [I would] refute every tongue that accuses [me]" (Isaiah 54:17).

As soon as you make some progress in reconciliation, the devil will rear his ugly head. You'll be doing just fine and something in the relationship will sour. Try not to terminate the relationship because of this. Anything worth attaining will involve some form of suffering. Let's not be ignorant of the devil's devices. Again, exercise wisdom in all dealings.

When reconciling, a host of people in your life will be surprised when you begin to interact with different races of people. You may be ridiculed, persecuted and probably forsaken. But is that going to stop you? What are you made of? We are the righteousness in Christ Jesus and according to Psalm 1:3, "like a tree planted by streams of water, which yields its fruit in season and whose leaf does not wither. Whatever he does prospers."

Although the disciples were surprised, they had spent enough time with Jesus to know better than to speak against the Lord. This is the same when you reconcile. If you are truly sent from God and you are representing His kingdom, "then no harm will befall you, no disaster will come near your tent" (Psalm 91:10). When they try to hurl any attacks they will realize that the Scripture reference, Psalm 105:15, "Do not touch my anointed ones; do my prophets no harm," applies to you.

I learned the hard way that you don't have to tell all of your business. It may come back to haunt you one day. Besides, what is your motivation for telling it? Do you want everyone to see how great you are? Or are your motives as pure as the driven snow? If they are, keep the personal details of your business to yourself. God will richly reward you.

I remember how painful it was for me when I adopted my special needs daughter. The Christians I shared the news with wounded me by offering comments like, "Don't you have enough to worry about with your biological children? Why would you do this to yourself?" Although my only motives were to honor the Lord in this, I shouldn't have sought man's approval. After all, my instructions were from Him. *When the Lord tells you to do something, don't stand around and wait for the rest of the world to embrace your vision. They may never catch it.*

Jesus will literally make all of our enemies our footstool. I vividly remember when I purchased my last home. The previous owners were professing bigots and strongly felt I wasn't worthy of their home. In fact I had to purchase it without ever seeing it. In the bureaucratic process, there was something I had no control over that delayed our closing. When we arrived at closing they were so angry with me that they literally were planning to sue me for damages. Right in the middle of closing I pulled out my Bible and began reading all the passages from the Psalms that dealt with my enemies being my footstool.

Well the short of it is, by the time I received the keys and moved into the house they had left me a riding mower, all swimming pool equipment, firewood, trash containers and the stickers, and window treatments. I know God honored my ability to ignore their threats and read the Bible without entertaining any hostility towards them. I had favor and protection from Him. I am sure they had no idea why they were doing all of this for me. "When a man's ways are pleasing to the Lord, he makes even his enemies live at peace with him" (Proverbs 16:7).

In verse 27 we also know that the disciples were more interested in food. There will be a time when you will stand alone. All your friends will be interested in pursuing more tangible relationships than cross-cultural ones. Don't get distracted by their lack of interest. Perhaps they aren't called to this task. Just honor the Lord and obey him. "Let us not become weary in doing good, for at the proper time we will reap a harvest if we do not give up" (Galatians 6:9).

In verse 28 the woman left her water jar and returned to her town. She was so preoccupied with the good news of Jesus that she left her prized possession. In reconciling you will be so excited about what the Lord is doing in your new relationship that you will no longer be preoccupied with life as usual. The Lord will open your eyes and give you a new revelation about Him.

In verse 29 she told the people to come and see a man who told her everything she ever did. In reconciling you may feel like you are born again. Remember when you first came to Christ how you wanted to evangelize the world? How you would tell everyone about Jesus? Well in reconciliation you will experience fervency in telling everyone about your new relationship. The enthusiasm for interacting cross-culturally will exude from your pores. So go for it!

In summation, Jesus was intentional, humble, compassionate and caring towards the Samaritan woman as He sought to reconcile with her. We need to do the same! Imagine if Jesus lived on earth in the twenty-first century. Perhaps this story would translate into Him walking into a gang-infested public housing project where He would probably befriend an African-American single mother.

In reconciliation we must adopt the techniques Jesus espoused in this Scripture passage. We must first offer living water, secondly we need to awaken a conscience, and thirdly we should lay down our lives for our fellow brothers and sisters in Christ.

Now that you have a biblical basis to strategize your first encounter let's role play:

Role Play Exercise

Directions: In your small group assign each member one of the roles described below and take five minutes per scenario to role-play this meeting. Make sure each individual plays the opposite of his or her race.

- Caucasian man approaching an African-American man
- An African-American woman approaching a Caucasian single mother
- A Caucasian male entrepreneur approaching an African-American college graduate
- A Caucasian woman approaching an African-American couple after a church service
- An African-American male approaching a Caucasian parolee
- A Caucasian married couple approaching an African-American married couple
- An African-American man approaching a Caucasian man

How would the above meeting transpire in these environments?

- Health club
- Church
- Grocery store
- Restaurant
- Doctor's office
- Theater
- Parking lot
- Community event

Strategies for Racial Reconciliation

Directions: Read John 4:4-30. Please write your own plan for reconciliation for this month.

Who are you planning to approach?

How will you approach them?

Where will you implement this plan?

What is your plan of action?

Do you intend to include anyone else in this plan? If so, who? Why did you choose them?

What Scripture reference will you meditate on to assist you on this journey?

What will be your strategy for coping if your plan doesn't materialize as you envisioned?

After the Initial Meeting

Directions: After the initial meeting, answer the following.

How was the experience?

What was your biggest surprise concerning the meeting?

What were some of the challenges?

What were your expectations?

What were their expectations?

What were your preconceived ideas about this person?

What were their preconceived ideas about you?

Were any stereotypes reinforced?

What stereotypes were dispelled?

Were your ideas about this person accurate?

Were their ideas about you accurate?

What is your next step concerning this friendship?

Would you ever pursue another opportunity similar to this one?

Chapter Five

The Church Model of Reconciliation

Since we've examined the model of reconciliation from the Bible's perspective let's now compare how the twenty-first century churches are doing in this race.

The first model of churches that came about during the pre-civil rights era was the segregated church. Religious segregation was characterized as a period when African Americans were prohibited from worshipping in Caucasian churches. The most fundamental reason for this was the belief they were inferior. This segregation not only occurred in the mainstream churches, but the Nation of Islam leaders began to publicly justify their own separation by saying it was God-ordained.

In these types of churches even the leaders who may not have agreed still went along with the program because they didn't want to lose their position. The only way a change was going to occur was if those who supported segregation were removed or changed their minds. Although today we rarely hear about overt cases of African Americans being denied entrance, there is more of a covert suggestion implied when you attend a church and you can sense you are not entirely welcome. Personally, I've attended churches in a region that is supposedly known as the Bible belt where I would have received a warmer reception from the Ku Klux Klan. *Neutrality is advantageous to the oppressor. Silence is an indictment in the crime of racism. And anyone who doesn't speak against it should be charged as an accessory.*

The second type of church model is the "non-partisan" church. This type focuses on trying to not attract different ethnic groups to their church. It is motivated by fear that "if we do, we will have to relinquish our unique style of worship." The biggest challenge I have with this church is their assumption that their style of worship is correct! Where did they get that idea from? In actuality they are merely a branch of the segregated church.

I attended one of these churches recently. The environment is completely sterile. It is so intellectually stimulating that I found myself needing to carry my concordances and Bible commentaries. The music is all classical and hymnals sung in monotone. It reminded me of something heard from the middle ages. It lacks cultural relevancy. There is absolutely no regard for diversity. I don't think they ever gave a second thought to possibly accommodating anyone else who didn't fit their prototype.

Since I am not a betting woman, I am willing to treat you to a cup of coffee at Starbucks that if they modified their music, invited African-American pastors to teach (I am probably pushing the envelope a little here), if they would hire at least one African-American individual on their staff in a position of leadership, just maybe their church will become a diverse body of believers.

The third type of church model is the assimilation model. This occurs when the doors are wide open for anyone to attend. However, when visitors arrive they have to adopt the culture already in attendance. There is no attempt to change the musical style or address the needs of the African-American community, or other cultures, from the pulpit. And no one is remotely interested in hiring an African American even if it means that individual serving in a menial position.

This group is expected to fit into the mold. They must become like the rest of the people already there (buckle-up-and-stay-in-your-place mentality) There are no attempts at allowing the incoming group to share their cultural distinctiveness. Keep in mind no one is immune from this type. It also occurs in predominantly African-American churches as well.

The problem with this type of church occurs when other cultural groups are present. There may be a time where the main culture tries to accommodate them. In doing so they may bill the service as a special event as opposed to making it an ongoing, integral part of the church worship service.

Another aspect of this model is when an ethnic church body is invited to share the same facility. This is okay as long as you allow that church body to share in the power and decision-making authority in the church. Sometimes this model is needed temporarily, for example, if the attendees have a language barrier and need a translator. It is also effective when the parishioners don't feel comfortable sharing their faith with the majority cultural. By all means try to accommodate their needs foremost. For example there may be Spanish speaking congregants who don't know the English language and are uncomfortable with worshipping with the majority culture. Their salvation is more important than man misjudging your deeds. The Lord will bless your efforts. Only He can judge your motives. He looks at our hearts. This model is temporary. The moment the parishioners become comfortable and are able to speak the language you may try combining both worship services.

The unfortunate part of this model is the church is viewed as operating an entertainment entity. Representation becomes the focus rather than reconciliation. This is already done at educational institutions. The goal here should be to integrate not to assimilate. Biblical reconciliation should have the goal of making us all equal in Jesus Christ. We should all be sharing His same power and authority. We should be celebrating our similarities while embracing our uniqueness.

The fourth style is the intentional model. This one seeks to intentionally recruit members of another group through creating a musical style of worship and preaching that will attract African Americans. This model recognizes African Americans as being on equal footing with the dominant culture. This church realizes that for every Caucasian speaker they pay an honorarium to there is an equally qualified African-American speaker that could bring forth the Word of God.

One of the disadvantages of this model is there can be an unconscious awareness to differentiate between the races and, for the sake of unity, issues may not be addressed openly through truth and love. For example, I visited a church that was racially mixed. It was almost a 50/50 split (what an amazing concept!) Anyway, the members all coexisted peacefully until a local political campaign entered the picture. It seemed like the majority of members were in favor of the Republican candidate while the minorities favored the Democratic candidate. What a rift this caused in the community. It nearly caused a church split. The problem occurred when the church supported the Republican candidate over the Democratic one. In this case it would have been wise if the church had taken a neutral stance. I've learned from this experience that all political controversies should be for individual consciences and not religious platforms.

The devil can use any of these strategies to prevent us from attaining racial harmony. In these instances the latter model is probably the most effective. Reconciliation doesn't require that we unite by negating our differences. We can still have our own identities and be unified. It is done every day in marriages. It is not peripheral or evangelical. It is not just another political agenda for radicals. It's an intentional quest at realizing that racism won't ever disappear unless we pursue it diligently. It's like making a marriage work. It requires wisdom, discernment, self-control and discipline.

It isn't until we recognize that racism needs to be addressed from the pulpits on Sunday mornings that we will ever see healing occur. When reconciling, your guide book is the Bible. You will find every single answer to life contained in the pages of Genesis through Revelation. You will find that even perplexing questions will be answered with parables and life stories from the many interesting personalities in the Bible.

Remember, those of us in leadership will be held accountable for our actions. Is your church leadership doing the best job they know how towards becoming a racially diverse congregation? If yes, what are they doing? (Contact me at agapeproductions@sbcglobal.net.) We are always interested in hearing from God's people about strategies that work. If no, what are you prepared to communicate to assist them? Are their actions lining up with God's Word?

In order for the church to be effective in racial reconciliation the leadership will have to set a good example for the rest of the body. Everyone should be on one accord when you discuss strategies on how to diversify the congregation. This will require that the pastoral leadership, music team, drama director, elders, deacons, teachers, lay ministers, service ministries, and even the food service staff sit down together and plan the most effective approach for the desired goal. As leaders, when attempting to reconcile, we must first define what the missions statement of our church looks like.

What is your church's mission statement?

Does it include reconciling cross-culturally?

What is your church's model?

If it is different from the intentional model, are the leaders aware of this disparity?

What are your plans for enlightening your church regarding this?

Are you uncomfortable about approaching anyone in leadership?

According to Matthew 18:15-17, what mandates do we have as Christ followers? Summarize the passage and elaborate:

According to Ephesians 2:11-22, what model should your church embrace? Summarize the passage and elaborate:

If you are in a church that doesn't embrace the vision for racial reconciliation, the mission is not impossible. Your current assignment if you accept it is to pray and ask the Holy Spirit to convict them and to wait patiently for the change to occur while quietly making a difference in your family and in your local community.

Chapter Six

Whites Only!

We will confine our solution to ten steps. I am sure there are more but for practical purposes let's begin with these.

A professional drag racer must prepare for a race. He cannot simply get into a car that isn't adequately prepared for the task. The engine and all its parts must be examined to ensure their proper function. Water, oil, and other fluids must be added, tires may need rotating, and the body of the car must be inspected. More importantly the racer needs to make sure he is wearing his helmet and proper equipment to guard against any fire hazards. He needs to wear a seat belt to protect him against any accidents that may occur. Once all of these precautions are in place he can set out on his race.

Here are a few preparations we as conciliators can adopt. Some of you have begun these approaches, so go to the head of the class.

Step #1—Acknowledge there is a problem. To be aware of the need for racial reconciliation and to not do anything about it is worse than racism itself. Racism is alive and well contrary to popular opinion. It does exist in the twenty-first century. No longer can we say that hostilities against our race are isolated events of white bigots. Just tune into the news and read the headlines. Wasn't it just a handful of years ago when an African-American male was beaten mercilessly by a Caucasian police officer? What about the former governor of Illinois having to commute the death sentences of many innocent men and women on death row who just happen to be mostly African Americans? Because the criminal justice system is unfairly prosecuting them because many of them don't have access to affordable legal assistance. The pandemic of AIDS in Africa and the United States is also the results of a lack of financial resources to access medicine in the African American community. Not to mention inferior public schools, joblessness and poverty highly representative in our communities? Still not convinced? Have you counted Chief Executive Officers who are African American who lead Fortune 500 companies? How about the disparity in college graduation for African Americans in the educational system?

In order to reconcile you must understand our pain. Without this ability your attempts at becoming our friends are doomed to fail. Try not to embrace the past-is-behind-you-mentality. That does absolutely nothing but alienate us even further. Stereotyping, racial profiling, prejudice and discrimination are in full operation. The inalienable rights of life, liberty and the pursuit of happiness remain to be seen by many African Americans. If you are of Caucasoid ancestry, it may be easy for you to view racism from a detachment mode. From this viewpoint it makes it easy to deny the reality of racism. In contrast, if you are an African American your view of racism is from a perspective of your own personal and familial experiences.

We all have heard the cliché that if you are not a part of the solution you are part of the problem. And just like Alcoholic Anonymous encourages their clients to admit they have a problem before they can solve it, we will never eradicate racism if we don't acknowledge it. You may sit back and say, "That's not my problem. I like African-American people. I am not prejudiced." Again, how many African-American friends do you have? The Bible speaks specifically about friendships. In order to have a friend you have to be a friend. Take the initiative to make friends with an African American. I haven't come across an individual yet who would resist a free cup of coffee or a meal. If your motives are pure and are clearly communicated, the possibilities are endless.

I would like to caution you just to be careful that you are not patronizing anyone. We are not ministry projects or tokens. We are God's children just like every other race He fearfully and wonderfully made. We have emotions and souls. God will certainly hold you accountable for your actions. While we are on the subject of accountability, please don't tell us how intelligent we are because we can enunciate. My Caucasian friends tell me that I am a very articulate and educated black woman who is not like most black people. They ask if I attended Yale or Harvard. I politely and with great restraint ask them what they mean by "most black people," because surely that has not been my experience. Usually the most courageous of the group will specify, "You know, the type that live in the ghetto." To which I reply, "Every culture has a sub-group of individuals whose dialectic may differ from the majority. Perhaps you are familiar with the people of the Appalachian Mountains. If you heard them speak you would be amazed how different their language sounds from yours even though they are Caucasians also."

For me to speak in complete sentences and utilize the correct grammatical form including nouns, adverbs, pronouns and adjectives would never be an issue of concern if I had been of Caucasian ancestry.

After you acknowledge there is a problem, repent! This is always something we need to change in our lives, whether it is possessing a hateful attitude, or resentment of others in words, actions or indifference.

As a Caucasian Christ follower, you may need to repent from your own arrogance of thinking you are a superior race. To think you are better than anyone else is the very rotten core of racism. Our sinful nature convinces us that because of our mere birth into a particular race, we should be proud. But to be proud of something none of us had any control over with is wrong. Ethnocentrism is a sin. Remember God hates pride with a passion because He knows how devastating it can be to man. We have to crucify our egos, because it is the very nature of our being to think we are God's gift to humanity. Racism is the effect of a disproportionate ego and the result of an individual's response to the world around them. As a man thinketh, so is he. If I live in a culture that tells me I am so wonderful because of my skin color, I am placed on a pedestal. We need to literally reprogram ourselves to see that we are members of one race—the human race.

Repentance involves the ability to forgive. You cannot have one without the other. We have to relieve ourselves of unresolved hurts and wounds. Many wounds are very deep. We can no longer be content with placing a bandage on the wound because the scar is still there when we remove it. We have to ask the Lord to completely heal us. When we petition His throne concerning reconciliation, He hears us.

There is something freeing about humbling yourself in the sight of God and man I cannot describe. Even if you are not contrite about what your forefathers did, you can still feel sympathy. I personally don't support the philosophy that Caucasians have to apologize to us unless of course they really want to. You cannot be held responsible for the sins of your fathers. However, you are responsible to make sure you are in right standing with the Lord concerning your attempts to reconcile cross-culturally.

If you're not motivated to make a formal apology, you can at least express a heartfelt sorrow over what was done to us. Look at Nehemiah and Daniel in the Old Testament, and how when they repented for their ancestors' sin the Lord blessed them. Can you stand a blessing?

Step #2 — Be sensitive to our plight. Just because you've never personally perpetrated or experienced a negative encounter with an African-American individual doesn't necessarily mean one hasn't occurred. That's like telling your doctor your leg isn't broken because there's no pain, when he has a set of x-rays supporting his claim. How many doctors would allow you to walk out of their office without being treated? I guarantee, if you oppose their efforts they will have you sign a liability wavier releasing them from a malpractice suit if you deny treatment.

Another example of this is, before I had children, whenever I would see a child misbehaving in public, I would be very judgmental and think, "Why doesn't that mother or father discipline their child?" I would think that if I had five minutes alone with that child I would get them in shape (yeah right!). My viewpoint changed when my children arrived.

We really cannot sympathize with someone unless we have experienced the same situation. And since God created you the way you are, you probably will never be able to fully appreciate an African American's plight until you have walked a mile in their moccasins.

As I said before, try not to patronize us. I am offended when you ask me to do a soul handshake, especially since I do not know how it's done. If you invite me over for dinner, simply serve whatever you usually prepare for your family. Don't prepare me what you think is a soul-food dinner, especially since that cuisine associated with our heritage is full of salt, fats and starches. I am learning how to eat healthy. Can I tell you about a Caucasian friend who brought to a potluck supper black-eyed peas who was greatly offended because none of the African Americans ate any? Her comment was, "I am surprised none of you tasted the meal I prepared." I responded by telling her that she made an inaccurate assumption based on our race that we would like black-eyed peas. It was quite an interesting lesson for us. She did repent and asked us what foods we liked with a promise to bring those for our next gathering.

If you are a Caucasian female, please don't ask me to braid your hair. That is why I pay my hair stylist $350 for my hairstyle. And if you are curious about my hair, please don't touch it as if I am an animal on display. That greatly offends me. And while I am on a roll, when you get a suntan don't make comments like, "I know how you feel being black now because I am almost as black as you," because frankly your skin color will change back at sundown.

When in doubt about how to act around us, pray and ask the Lord for wisdom.

Step #3 — Please don't overcompensate. Don't have good intentions that simply do more harm than good. I can recall one of my Caucasian friends who along with her husband decided they would reach out to an African-American single parent. Their frame of reference had them thinking they should treat her like a daughter instead of another sister in the Lord, and, since the young woman was already experiencing multiple losses in her life, she thought it was a great idea. Around $20,000 later they realized what they had done. It wasn't that *she* committed a crime; it was the couple who had defined their relationship to her as parental. How many of us would not ask our parents to help us if we were in need? This couple overcompensated. The best thing to do in these circumstance is to define your limitations up front so both parties will be clear and have sound expectations of what will occur.

I am happy to report this story had a happy ending. The couple redefined their relationship with her and both sides are enjoying a relationship with the proper boundaries established. So try not to overcompensate with us and, as I have said, make sure your actions are not motivated by guilt.

Additionally, if you are planning to initiate relationships with us, make sure they are lifetime commitments that have a chance to mature. If you are just interested in having an African American in your life because it is politically correct, please do us no favors. God will reveal to us the motives of your heart. Don't hire us unless we are qualified for the job. If you do, you will set us up for failure and you will be responsible for perpetuating more racial strife and division. If you own a corporation don't use us as if we are some chattel for a tax break. Slavery was abolished a long time ago. I *am* a staunch advocate for affirmative action, but only when the individual is the most qualified for the job.

Please don't deny us entrance to country clubs. Even as rich as Tiger Woods and Michael Jordan are, they are still not permitted into certain country clubs in certain areas of the world. They may be legally allowed to enter, but that doesn't necessarily ensure the doormat says "welcome."

In your effort to relate to us, please don't try to emulate what behavior you think is characteristic of our people. I absolutely despise entering the car of a Caucasian person who automatically assumes I like rap music. I hate rap with a passion. I don't listen to derogatory music. When someone makes assumptions about me based on my race it offends me greatly. Frankly I only enjoy classical, country western and sacred music. Please don't try to sound "black," whatever that means. Don't emulate lingo that I would absolutely have no idea where it came from. Besides, I have a difficult time trying to decipher what language my teenagers are speaking. Just relate to me as a sister in Christ, not to my ethnicity. Because I promise you, we are all as different as you are and operate with different gifts and abilities. So if you try to force us into some prototype, you will be greatly disappointed.

When you invite us out for dinner, please don't assume we haven't experienced fine dining. I do know which utensils to use (and even if I didn't, I would emulate what everyone else was using.) If you are courageous enough to ask me over for dinner at your home you don't have to impress me. I can enjoy a meal on paper plates. Whenever you talk about your vacations, you don't have to speak to me condescendingly. I have traveled extensively throughout the world and have probably been to many of the places you are referring to.

Please don't assume that because I am African American and have a quiver full of children I am impoverished. Can I tell you a quick story? Thanks. A few years ago my daughter's school called and said, "Mrs. Heckler, this is Con Descending (name changed to protect the not-so-innocent). Every year at this time in cooperation with the local churches we give gifts to the needy families of our communities and your name came up." Before she could utter another word I cut her completely off and said, "I would love to give a donation. How much do you need?"

How dare she assume that we were a needy family based on our size and heritage! We have never presented ourselves as being in dire need of anything. She made three false assumptions based on my race, marital status and amount of children. I couldn't help but wonder if I had been a single Caucasian mother with five children would she still have extended me the same offer? How dare she make such assumptions! And before you accuse me of not being grateful, if she wanted to extend grace to our family there were proper ways to accomplish this. She could have sent an anonymous invitation through the mail and allowed me to respond if I felt I was in need. I am not oversensitive. I'm just a little annoyed.

Step #4—Be proactive in your quest to reconcile. Be intentional, take risks. Be the first one to initiate friendships with African-American people. We all harbor fears of rejection at some time in our lives whether it's with male or female relationships or in the marketplace. You may possibly face criticism or humiliation. So what? Remember what Jesus Christ suffered at the hands of His own people. Certainly you know that you are in no way greater than Him. So let's approach this from His perspective. You want to be like Jesus more and more each day, right? Well, start by reconciling like He did!

Remember the old adage nothing ventured noting gained? If each one of us waits for the other person to initiate the friendship process, it may never occur. It is not enough to say that you have an African-American friend who ends up just being a coworker. Why not invite him or her to your church? Or to your home? Do you know their children or where they are from? Seek out a natural desire to be with them. Try to become very comfortable being in their presence.

Make the first move. For example, if you are in a restaurant and you see an African American waiting for a table, maybe you can begin a conversation by saying, "The food must really be great here since we have to wait so long." Hopefully they will respond and you can take the conversation from there. Whenever you find yourself in your daily routine, ask God to give you an ordained opportunity to cross paths with an African American who would be open to establishing a true friendship with you.

In attempting to reconcile cross-culturally, pray. It will be the most effective tool you'll need on your journey. When you answer the call to be used as an instrument for God's purposes, you will naturally feel inadequate. That is because you are. We are all nothing without Him. Ask the Lord for His mercy and grace. All you need is a heart after Him, wisdom, discernment, humility and a teachable spirit. Remember the Lord has your best interest at heart. Don't place your confidence in man. Man will let you down every time. Apply Proverbs 3:5-6 to your life. "Trust in the Lord with all your heart and lean not on your own understanding; in all your ways acknowledge him, and he will make your paths straight."

After the Lord reveals to you His plan for approaching someone, be prepared for rejection. Be prepared for distrust. Anyone would be suspicious when suddenly a person they never met before wants to take them out to dinner. If you are initially rejected don't give up. Try to be honest. Tell the individual what your motives are. If you are married make sure your spouse is involved with the interaction so that you avoid any miscommunication. For example, when church is over if you see an individual from a different culture standing in the lobby, you may say something like this, "Hello. My name is John and my small group is meeting tonight for dinner at the Cheesecake Factory and I was wondering if you would be interested in joining us?" The individual will either say yes or no. If they say no usually they will give some excuse as to why they cannot attend. So don't take it personally. Just politely thank them and say, "Maybe some other time." If they accept your dinner invitation, make it as comfortable for them as possible by saying, "Here are the directions" or "Would you like to follow us in your car?"

When you arrive at the restaurant continue to make them comfortable by relieving them from the anxiety of worrying about who will pick up the check. You can say something like, "Thank you for being our guest. You can order anything you would like; it's our treat." After you feed them you may have earned yourself a new friend. More importantly you have pleased the Lord.

I recall when I was serving at church, a couple from Germany approached me in the foyer and introduced themselves. They asked me about the church and its operation and about the theology. I was totally surprised when they offered to take me out to dinner after I had recommended a good pizza restaurant. And the only reason I didn't go was because I had a prior commitment. Of course we have safety issues in today's society and I would have insisted that I drive in my own car and made sure it was a public place where I met them. However, I was so pleased about the invitation that I promise you I would have attended. Good for them!

Sometimes in our fervor to reconcile we try to force relationships upon meeting the individual. It is not important when befriending someone that you learn their entire life story during the first meeting, especially if you are reconciling with non-believers. I can assure you that if they are not in Christ they will have quite a story to tell. Don't insist on intimate details. As your friendship develops they will begin to open up. Remember, not every interaction will lead to a new relationship. Some of us sow seeds, some of us water, some of us fertilize and yet others of us are reapers. You may rarely see the fruit of your labors on this side of heaven. Nevertheless you are charged with the command to go. If there are no fruitful results in a reasonable amount of time, don't sweat it. Keep trying!

Step #5—Release the save-the-world-mentality. I mentioned this earlier, but I'll go into a little more depth here. Always seek to initiate an equal partnership with African Americans. We are not looking for a Savior. We already have one. Jesus gave His life for all of humanity. We are all equal at the foot of the cross. We don't need pity or handouts. Please don't move back into our neighborhoods after you have already left because you want to bring economic stability. Move in because you genuinely want to live side by side with us. My first experience with "white flight" was as a nine-year-old living in Ohio. I was devastated that my neighbor, whose daughter was my best friend, in the middle of the night made their getaway and never said good-bye to us. It took me more than ten years to heal from that pain. I live near a major US city and I am amazed how Caucasians are moving back to the inner city, driving up the real estate value as the minorities are being forced to move to the Southern states where the cost of living is less expensive. Please don't misinterpret me—there is nothing wrong with Caucasians returning to the inner city. My point is it should not force African-American or Hispanic people out of the community. The local government should have some type of program to assist individuals with fewer resources to continue to live side by side with our Caucasian brother's and sister's.

When attempting to be used by God, don't broadcast your good deeds. You know what the Bible says about that. According to Matthew 6:2-4, "'So when you give to the needy, do not announce it with trumpets, as the hypocrites do in the synagogues and on the streets, to be honored by men. I tell you the truth, they have received their reward in full. But when you give to the needy, do not let your left hand know what your right hand is doing, so that your giving may be in secret. Then your Father, who sees what is done in secret, will reward you.'"

It's the same when reconciling cross-culturally. Whenever you plan to minister to the African-American community first of all ask them if you can help. Please don't assume that you are always welcome even if you are providing some financial assistance. Ask if you can serve in a certain manner. If the recipients are open to it, please take other African Americans you are in partnership with to serve with you. There is nothing more aggravating to us than to see a group of well-meaning white people get off of a bus to come into our neighborhood for a few hours and then return to their safe, rich, and well-lighted communities. Remember, those people you are intending to serve should be invited when you are planning.

If you are mentoring a child, please make a lifetime commitment if possible, or at least two to five years. You will do more damage if you establish a relationship for a few months then figure out that you are too busy to continue. Don't start something you cannot finish. Let your motivation for all good deeds be out of your love for Christ. Remember that, according to Numbers 30:2, "When a man makes a vow to the Lord or takes an oath to obligate himself by a pledge, he must not break his word but must do everything he said."

Step #6 — Don't expect us to assimilate into mainstream society. In order for the melting pot stew to have great flavor, we must season it with a wide variety of spices. The goal here is not to assimilate us into the mainstream culture, it should be to integrate, with the idea of identifying different heritages while simultaneously allowing each group to maintain their own unique culture.

We are not required to assimilate into society and conform to the establishment. African Americans, as a race of people, have our own unique gifts and talents. Just look at the way we have significantly contributed to the world. Look how we revolutionized the fashion industry. Urban clothing came from our culture. Look at the music we created, not to mention how our musical style was borrowed from us. Musical artists like Elvis Presley and the Beatles created billion-dollar conglomerates based on a distinct musical style associated with our church community. How entertaining it is for me to see Hollywood women inject collagen into their lips to make them fuller—a characteristic God so graciously gave to African-American women. I can never fully understand how some Caucasians can ridicule our complexion yet spend endless hours in the sun trying to darken their skin.

We shouldn't be expected to absorb mainstream values either. We have our own morality that is characteristic of our culture. For example, we are taught at a very early age to respect our elders. That means anyone over twenty-one years old is usually addressed as sir or ma'am. Senior citizens in our community are addressed as mother or father, whether they gave birth to us or not. We even have respect for our peers. My friends' children call me Auntie Kandis and my children do the same for her and her spouse. It's just a cultural thing. I cannot explain it.

Another characteristic within our community is we are staunch disciplinarians for the most part—there are certainly exceptions to every rule—but generally speaking, an African-American mother takes nothing off her children. I've seen us in public, backhand a whining child, irrespective of the consequences. Before I adopted my youngest son I had tremendous challenges, because the foster care system prohibited any type of corporal punishment. And he knew it. So whenever we would be out in public he would perform. The grocery store was a battlefield. But as soon as I signed on the dotted line I took him into the bathroom and with the rod of correction, applied it to the county seat. After a couple of those, I never had another incident in public. All you have to do as an African-American mother is give your children a look when they are misbehaving that communicates "I will knock you into next week if you don't stop." My mother's favorite line was "I brought you into this world and I will take you out." Of course that statement isn't totally theologically sound. I tell my children, "In cooperation with the Lord I brought you into this world, and the Bible tells me, according to Proverbs 22:15, 'Folly is bound up in the heart of a child, but the rod of discipline will drive it far from him.'"

I thank God daily for my African-American parents who instilled in me great values, worth and a very healthy self-esteem. There is nothing on earth I cannot accomplish because of them. I remember always grumbling because I had to be in before the street lights came on. But those boundaries assisted me with becoming the woman I am today. Not only did I learn how much my parents loved me by imposing curfews, but the greater lesson was I learned to love myself and not to tolerate any relationships that would compromise my integrity or the respect I had for myself.

The African proverb that states "it takes a whole village to raise a child" is one of our strongest attributes. We are very communal. Years ago in our communities if my children were seen misbehaving, my neighbors would spank them first and then bring them home where they would be spanked again. But with all of the laws today associated with child abuse, this practice has become extinct. How I long for the olden days.

We are also multigenerational. If you've ever attended a family reunion in our community you will witness interaction between grandparents, parents, toddlers, teens and young adults. You will see a gray-haired man throwing a ball to a toddler and an older woman who can barely walk running in a potato-sack race with her teenage grandson.

Our communities are very strong units. I can recall more than two decades ago when a family from my former church had a fire that destroyed their home. How refreshing it was to see the community respond in less than twenty-four hours to all of their needs. By the end of the week the Lord had restored a hundredfold what they had lost.

We are also very compassionate people who identify with the lost, hurt and the broken. We are empathetic to their condition primarily because of all we have endured in our lives. We are extremely passionate about our Lord. We consider ourselves favored people because of our ability to survive. We love our Lord with such great fervency that our Sunday morning worship services are usually emotionally charged.

Have you ever attended an African-American Sunday worship service? If you haven't you should. You are in for an experience of a lifetime. Just make sure you take along a sack lunch because our services generally last three hours. I've recently attended one and this is what I observed. The service began with a devotion. There were three deacons who stood before the church who opened up with an old hymn they didn't know. They sang it off-key and very loud. The older mothers were dressed in white from head to toe and sat on the front pews. The second oldest deacon read a Scripture passage for about five minutes. As he mispronounced a few words, the teenage girls in the very back row laughed hysterically. The climax of devotion time occurred when the third deacon prayed for his personal needs and talked about how the devil was with him last night but he got the victory. As a few mothers in the front pew said amen, others nodded off to sleep. The preschool children in the middle pews began to squirm. After a ten-minute prayer, one of the deacons began to signal that the devotion should be drawn to a close.

Immediately following the devotion, the choir director walked in with the full attention of the congregation. As the music loudly began he engaged in a dramatic presentation of worship, raising his hands as his entourage marched in on beat. The choir's footsteps were all in sync like a military drill team at basic training. Like a maestro conducting a symphony, the choir director encouraged melodious harmony in praises to the Lord. After five selections and renditions of songs that lasted several minutes each, the director concluded on a falsetto note that lasted at least another twenty seconds. The song was received by a fierce round of applause and a standing ovation. He humbly bowed, wiped his head with a folded white towel and sat down.

As the choir director composed himself the pastor, with more pomp and circumstance than the choir director, pranced down the center aisle. The music roared again as the pastor read at least three pages of announcements from the church bulletin. After the announcements the Kentucky Fried Chicken offering buckets were passed to collect the tithes and offerings. Around 2:00 p.m. the pastor began to preach a sermon that lasted one and a half hours. The pastor, appearing to be emotionally exhausted, commanded his nurse in full white uniform to wipe his brow with a fancy white handkerchief. She also gave him a drink of water and stood there to protect him from the masses.

At the end of church there was fellowship with food featuring fried chicken and all the trappings of a Thanksgiving meal. I watched as every member actively engaged in conversation about their lives. We ate then ran back upstairs to start the worship service all over again.

So there you have it—my observations of an African-American worship service. But don't take my word for it. You will have to attend one of these services for yourself.

When I speak of assimilation I am not talking about a total rejection of societal morality and norms. Of course we have to submit in some areas to the values imposed by our society. There are rules, laws and customs that have to be followed to maintain order. No society could function properly without a set of mores and regulations governing human behavior. For example, we have to assimilate to a certain degree if we want employment. I couldn't tell you the numerous employment opportunities denied me because I didn't embody a certain persona. There were a few times when I called back and asked for feedback as to why I was denied a position. One of the Caucasian human resource clerks was honest enough to tell me the truth. She said she overheard them saying if I looked more mainstream I would have been hired. I knew exactly what she meant. That was the time when I had a militant hair style. It wasn't acceptable in the late 1970s to be black and proud in the workplace. I must admit I was a rebel with a cause.

So in order to be employed I swallowed my pride and changed my hairstyle. I bought a new suit. I toned down my jewelry and asked my best white girlfriend to role-play with me how to interview for a job. Two weeks later I was hired by a major oil company. In fact I was the youngest African-American employee in the history of the company. So theoretically if I hadn't assimilated I probably would not have received that employment opportunity.

Another example of assimilation is how we all follow the traffic laws. Can you imagine how chaotic our society would be if half of the population stopped at red lights and the other half didn't? We would be in serious trouble.

Our heritage is very rich. It is ingrained in us. Please don't expect us to change. We have customs, traditions and philosophies that make us who we are. Please accept us and celebrate who we are in Jesus Christ.

Step #7—Stand against any form of racism. Someone who laughs at a racially motivated joke at the water cooler at work is as offensive as the individual telling the joke. If you are riding on public transportation and an open seat is by an African American, why not sit next to the individual? If you work in human resources and an African American is just as qualified as his or her Caucasian counterpart, why not consider hiring them?

To purchase designer clothing when you are aware that part of the proceeds go to support the Ku Klux Klan is racism. To watch a television program where the characters are portraying African Americans negatively is racism. If you see an African American trying to purchase real estate next door to you and you encourage your neighbors not to sell to them because you think it will affect your property value that is racism. Or if they buy the house and you move out because you don't want to live next door to them that is racism. If you're in a restaurant and decide you don't want to sit next to an African-American family and ask for another seat that is racism. If you are a department store cashier and you follow an African American around the store as if they had stolen something that is racism. If you rent an African American an apartment over the phone and when they arrive in person you suddenly remember the apartment has been rented that is racism.

Hopefully by now you have gotten the point. Racism is never a gray area. It is always black and white, meaning if the motives of your heart are premeditated and you deliberately set out to harm someone you are exhibiting a racist attitude. Let's take the last circumstance and use it as an example of someone *not* being racist. You own an apartment complex and you have apartments available. An African American calls (you may not be aware of their ethnicity) and you tell them you do have some units available. After a preliminary telephone interview the individual appears as though they will work out. They gather all of their paperwork and come to your office, ecstatic about their new apartment. By the time they arrive you have completed a credit report on them and learned they have filed bankruptcy. Of course you cannot rent to them. Perhaps over the phone you could have specified, "Barring any unforeseen circumstances, should you have a favorable credit report and good references, you can have the unit." Are you following my logic? That would not be racism. But how would you be able to prove it in a court of law?

I am sure there are endless misunderstandings on the part of both races that could have been avoided if there was proper communication. Here's another example of misunderstanding due to lack of communication. Let's use the restaurant scenario. A Caucasian family enters a restaurant where an African-American family is already seated. The hostess brings the Caucasian family to the table situated next to the African American. After the Caucasian family sees the African Americans they decide they want to sit somewhere else. Now if you were the African-American family, what would you deduce? Exactly. This was a real experience for my family. If I had been the Caucasian family I would have at the very least looked at the African-American family, smiled and said, "We need a little more room because my daughter with her wheelchair is coming." I would have made an attempt to not offend them. Or I would have told the hostess to tell them that we wanted more privacy. Are you following me? Let's think before we act.

Step #8—Rest from your desire to rule. This concept is the most difficult one for most Caucasian men to grasp. The Lord made you that way. You have been conditioned all of your life to be protectors and providers. I love the concept of men being men. There is nothing more appealing to me than a very aggressive and strong man. From the days you were commanded by the Lord to work, you have always done your job extremely well. All I am trying to communicate is for you to share the power and share the wealth. Repent by giving up the reins of power and distribute the wealth equally with the rest of us. What good father who has several children will leave an inheritance to only one of his children? Why would you think our Daddy, Jesus, would not allow us to have the same inheritance as his other children? None of us are illegitimate. We are not asking for a handout. Just give us our fair share, considering how we built this country on slave labor and how we were responsible for many inventions everyone uses, such as computers, cell phones and golf tees. I would say just the invention of that golf tee alone should be worth its weight in gold!

Even though you may disagree with affirmative action, until you can create a viable solution for employing and educating us don't reject it. We're just asking for equal access! Let me clue you in on a little secret. Look at these prophetic events that are occurring in our headlines. Take a moment to think about it. Look at the stock market, housing and the economy. I have at least a handful of friends who are affected by unemployment. How long do you think our Lord is going to allow us to be denied economic stability? It's not going to happen. So let's begin to disburse the funds and give us our fair share now.

You can count the corporations that are grossing more than 55 million dollars a year where African Americans are the Chief Executive Officers, on one hand. On one finger you can't even count the Fortune 500 companies owned exclusively by us. How pathetic that even sports celebrities and entertainers who are able to afford extravagant lifestyles, when they try to purchase sports teams or finance the productions they are starring in, frequently end up needing a Caucasian partner.

Real change will only occur when you give us equal access to housing, medical resources, social services, educational and economic resources.

Please do not buy into the reverse discrimination hype. In order for reverse discrimination to occur, whites would have to be oppressed for hundreds of years, would have to fight for their human rights, would have to be denied economic power, devalued, demeaned, abused and treated like they were inhuman. Has this happened?

In order for us to overcome, you will have to share the power and white privileges. It's a sacrifice. We've been doing it for years. It's your turn.

Step #9 —When seeking to begin new friendships with African Americans seek an environment of mutual respect. When dealing with oppressed people, you need to establish equal footing. To level the playing field try conversing about spiritual matters. We are all equal in the Lord's sight. But some people have been conditioned all of their lives to believe they are superior or inferior. For them it will take some serious spiritual warfare to break those chains of bondage. So while we wait for their breakthrough, we will engage them in conversations surrounding Christ and His kingdom. For example, you can lead by saying, "You know, I haven't seen you around here. How long have you been attending this church?" Engage them in a conversation about the Lord to assist in breaking any barriers. As African Americans we are very relational and usually prefer interacting with you on a familial level.

I am still amazed by some Caucasians attempts to relate to me by asking what I do for a living. What if the individual you are seeking to reconcile to is a sanitation worker and they are not proud of their job? How would it look if you as a Caucasian began talking about the million-dollar mark you just passed selling real estate? Or if you were engaging in a conversation about the cruise to Europe you are about to take next month, how do you expect that individual to relate to you? You have separated them even further by socioeconomic status now. Please use wisdom.

It wasn't until my sons attended a private high school where we live that I became aware of our socioeconomic status. For the most part I thought we were living well. We had all the trappings of a middle-class family. We were keeping up with the Joneses. It wasn't until they came home from school one day that I realized we were working class. They arrived all excited because their entire freshmen class was invited by one of the parents to visit their California summer home for spring break. The boys were especially thrilled because not only would they be treated to a week of easy living with servants at their disposal, but the parents would send their jet to transport their entire class. (I would feed a nation if I had that wealth.)

Of course, in this whole interaction I felt an object lesson was appropriate. I asked my sons when was the last time they saw a moving van at a cemetery, you can't take your money with you when you die. Only what they did for Christ and His kingdom would last. I told my boys they couldn't go.

Another instance occurred when I was confronted at my son's volleyball game by a well-intentioned parent trying to become better acquainted with me. Although I am a flaming extrovert and make friends very easily, I still try to keep a low profile. I have erected steel barriers that guard my heart concerning my personal business. I am just not the type of person who volunteers my entire life story at the drop of a hat, although many are glad to provide me with such information. So a very wealthy parent decided to share with me their latest acquisition and their recent trip to Paris. As I sat there totally oblivious to their faint attempts at impressing me they became rather annoyed.

She rattled on profusely most of the game. In order to provide myself with some relief I decided to participate. Well to her total dismay, I was able to speak in complete sentences and carry on in conversation. She was extremely impressed that I actually lived in the area where the school was located. She was also quite astonished to learn I had traveled extensively and had visited many of the same countries she had traveled to. I am always amazed at the presuppositions surrounding my life. How wrong people have been about me, and sometimes I must admit I've misjudged others a time or two.

I can't count the times the Federal Express driver arrived at my door and asked for the owner of the home. And the time I was about to make a presentation concerning my company and had to sit in the waiting room for more than an hour because they assumed I wasn't the Chief Executive Officer, even though I was dressed in business attire and introduced myself as such. I especially get a charge from the people who think I am German because of my last name and when I show up, they are overwhelmed with shock.

I've had my share of mistakes also. I remember meeting a millionaire who was a potential investor for my company and, based on his appearance, I asked him when Mr. Banks was arriving. Caucasians don't have a corner on the market for mistakes. If you're honest, you know we all make rash judgments about people that are incorrect.

After all the Bible tells us, "'Do not judge, and you will not be judged. Do not condemn, and you will not be condemned'"(Luke 6:37). So, as I was saying, when attempting to relate to us stay humble. We all have equal footing at the cross.

Step #10 — Set a good example for your children concerning racial reconciliation.

Modeling Reconciliation Survey

Directions: On a scale from 1-10, with 10 being the Jesus model of reconciliation, please rate yourself. Have you daily modeled a good witness for your children?

1. **Do you talk about current issues in the media that concern racism? What do you tell your children about the disproportionate amount of negative images in the media concerning African Americans?**

1 2 3 4 5 6 7 8 9 10

2. **When your children are watching a television program that degrades minority groups, do you turn the channel?**

1 2 3 4 5 6 7 8 9 10

3. **When your children talk about someone of a different race in a negative manner, do you speak up?**

1 2 3 4 5 6 7 8 9 10

4. **When they stereotype someone based upon their race, do you speak up?**

1 2 3 4 5 6 7 8 9 10

5. **If they want to be friends with an African-American individual, do you respond favorably?**

1 2 3 4 5 6 7 8 9 10

6. **If they want to date an African American, do you respond favorably?**

1 2 3 4 5 6 7 8 9 10

7. **How many friends do you have who are African American?**

1 2 3 4 5 6 7 8 9 10

8. **How many cultural activities have you attended within the past year?**

1 2 3 4 5 6 7 8 9 10

9. **How many African Americans have you hired within the last five years?**

1 2 3 4 5 6 7 8 9 10

10. **How many ministry outreach projects in the inner city did you take your children to last year?**

1 2 3 4 5 6 7 8 9 10

11. **How many African-American churches have you visited in the past month? How about in the past year?**

1 2 3 4 5 6 7 8 9 10

12. **How many times did you interact with an African American (other than a coworker) in the past year?**

1 2 3 4 5 6 7 8 9 10

13. **How much financial support have you given to African American causes within the past year?**
1 2 3 4 5 6 7 8 9 10

14. **How many lectures have you attended on African-American culture within the past year?**
1 2 3 4 5 6 7 8 9 10

15. **How many books have you read relating to African-American culture in the past month?**
1 2 3 4 5 6 7 8 9 10

16. **How many programs have you attended that celebrated African-American culture in the past year?**
1 2 3 4 5 6 7 8 9 10

17. **How many letters have you written to missionaries serving in predominately African-American communities this past year?**
1 2 3 4 5 6 7 8 9 10

18. **How many prisons have you visited this past year?**
1 2 3 4 5 6 7 8 9 10

19. **How many homeless people have you mentored this past year?**
1 2 3 4 5 6 7 8 9 10

20. **How often have you prayed for racial reconciliation this month?**
1 2 3 4 5 6 7 8 9 10

Racing Towards Reconciliation Plan

Directions: Write two steps you plan to implement this month in your race towards reconciliation. Each month write two more and report to your small group your progress. Make it a six-month goal to implement all ten steps.

1.

2.

3.

4.

5.

6.

7.

8.

9.

10.

Chapter Seven

Colored Only!

Allow me to make a disclaimer before we begin this chapter. I am not the spokesperson for the entire African-American race. We are about as different as the stars are in the sky. So please don't send me any letters or misquote me. I am only speaking for myself. I have to stand before the Lord alone one day and give an account for what I write and say.

Reconciliation is a double-edged sword for all of us because it requires change. All of our lives we have had to adapt to the dominant culture. In fact, our very survival depended on it. But if we expect our Caucasian brothers and sisters to change their ways, we are required to flex ourselves. No longer can we idly sit by and ask them to labor on our behalf. We are to collaborate with them and make their journey easier and more profitable. There are ten steps to assist us with reconciliation.

Step #1—Forgive the past. In Philippians 3:13-14 Paul states, "'Brothers, I do not consider myself yet to have taken hold of it. But one thing I do: Forgetting what is behind and straining toward what is ahead, I press on toward the goal to win the prize for which God has called me heavenward in Christ Jesus.'" Though Paul who was a notorious persecutor of Christians, he was able to forget his past. Paul spoke about our citizenship being in heaven. We can't dwell on the sins of their fathers—we don't have much time left before the rapture occurs. We need to focus all of our energy on kingdom-building and ensuring that we leave a legacy for the generations that follow us.

If we want to attain forgiveness for our own sins, we must not charge the sins of Caucasian people to an account. We must credit their statement every single time they offend us. Please don't ask me how many times according to Matthew 18:22 it is seventy-seven times, more than we can keep track of. Don't carry a chip on your shoulder and harbor any type of resentment. Remember it was some of their ancestors who mistreated us. They are only responsible for what they do to us today, and even at that the Lord will reward them according to their deeds.

We have to search our hearts and rid them of sin. It helps if we verbally confess. After acknowledging our faults to one another, we need to follow through on our actions and attitudes making sure they line up with the Word of God. It is also wise to have a partner who holds you accountable. Once we surrender to the Lord, He will be able to do good works in us.

We have our own issues in our community, and we need to forgive one another and ourselves for missing the mark. *We are enslaved again if we choose not to forgive.*

Step #2—Stop whining. The government owes us nothing. Stop relying on welfare that was created as a temporary solution to a financial crisis. Don't take advantage or misuse the system. Public Assistance was designed to assist, not to rely on, and should only be used as a stepping stone. We need to be grateful for what they have done for us already. We need to climb down from our laundry detergent boxes and stop playing the blame-the-white-people game. It's getting a little old. We've been using that one for over two hundred years. Don't get me wrong, racism is alive and well, but we have to admit we've come a long way, baby. We need to release the slavery mentality that forced us to be dependent on a system designed to enslave us even further. No more bondage to social welfare. Release the entitlement mentality. No one owes us anything. All groups of people since the dawn of creation have had adverse circumstances to endure. We've all had financial difficulties. So get over it. No more handouts. Stop complaining. Sometimes we can be our own worst enemy. Life is hard for everyone.

We must avoid using our race as an excuse for our own shortcomings. We've become adept at playing the race card. We can no longer make our Caucasian brothers and sisters feel guilty for their mistreatment of us. We have our own internal problems in our community which are based on demoralization which prevents us from empowering ourselves economically. We have a tendency to forget our gifts and fail to make the most of all the opportunities God grants us. Some of us have a parasite mentality where we latch on to someone and endlessly drain them.

Don't bite the hand that is feeding you. Be grateful. There are countless Caucasian men and women who have generously given of their time, money and resources to further God's kingdom on our behalf. There are more well-intentioned people on earth than we think. Let's not alienate them by treating them as if they are doing us a favor, because they really don't have to. There are other groups of people who would appreciate their beneficence. Look at the Hispanic people who risk their lives daily to sneak into this country. Observe how they take menial jobs to provide for their families. Watch how grateful they are living in this country.

Sometimes we are plagued by a lack of self-efficacy of the heart and mind. This may encourage us to adopt a fatalistic outlook that communicates, "I am not going to make it in this white-dominated society, so why should I try?" Sometimes we may be tempted to use our skin color as justification for not wanting to try harder. The victimization mentality is detrimental if we are trying to gain empowerment. We have to begin to take responsibility for our own actions.

Step #3—Vote on the issues, not on tradition. We cannot continue to vote based on traditions. Just because your great-granddaddy voted democratic doesn't mean you have to. Research what the candidates stand for. In the past we've been so busy electing a Democratic president we felt would keep all of our social programs intact, that we failed to recognize some flaws in his character. We were so preoccupied with our own needs that we allowed the presidential office of the United States of America to be disgraced. If you are a Christ follower, you must think from an entirely different perspective than the world. We are too intelligent to base our votes on social welfare.

We need to vote on candidates based on their integrity and character. At the time of this publication, we are right in the middle of a historical democratic presidential nomination of an African American. Please pray about who you think God would want in that office. I don't care about a lack of or too much experience, I want someone in there who shares my same values of pro-life and the sanctity of marriage. Someone who listens to the Lord before he makes a decision about war. Let's vote responsibly. And please vote. Our ancestors died so that we would have this privilege.

While I am on a roll, please do me a favor and don't equate Jesse Jackson and Louis Farrakhan with Moses and Joshua. They are not our saviors. We already have one named Jesus. These men are simply pushing their own political agendas. If you need a living example of racial reconciliation, read about the life of Jesus Christ.

The Nation of Islam is an organization that seeks to perpetuate the crime of racism. We need to dismiss any philosophies or ideologies that deviate from the Word of God. If they are not preaching Jesus Christ and Him crucified, raised from the dead and coming again, run. I don't care how many marches they hold or what contributions they make to the community, they are wrong! And the truth will set them free (John 8:32).

Regarding our economic status, please don't point the finger at anyone. Remember these conditions didn't occur overnight. Please don't speak irreverently of our president. The Lord has placed him in authority and we are supposed to govern ourselves accordingly. According to Romans 13:1-2, "Everyone must submit himself to the governing authorities, for there is no authority except that which God has established. The authorities that exist have been established by God. Consequently, he who rebels against the authority is rebelling against what God has instituted, and those who do so will bring judgment on themselves." Pray for our president.

Step #4—Let's serve our Caucasian brothers and sisters. For those Caucasian brothers and sisters who genuinely want a cross-cultural relationship with us, please assist them. Embrace them. Try not to walk in fear and mistrust. As they reach out to us extend the same hospitality towards them. If the relationship becomes turbulent as being human factors in, take some responsibility in correcting it. We have to begin trusting that they have our best interest at heart. Ask the Holy Spirit for wisdom to discern whether or not they do. We have to disciple, educate, accept them for who they are, and partner with them in this matter of reconciliation.

Let's not take offense to every misdeed done by our Caucasian brothers and sisters. The majority mean well. Let's not retaliate when they try to relate and end up offending us. Take the road less traveled. We won't make any progress if we hold bitterness, resentment and hostility towards them. There are times when righteous indignation is appropriate, but try to reserve those times for when overt racism is in full operation.

We need to have servants' hearts. How will we witness to our brothers and sisters in Christ if we don't live out Matthew 20:26-28 that states, "'Whoever wants to become great among you must be your servant, and whoever wants to be first must by your slave—just as the Son of Man did not come to be served, but to serve, and to give his life as a ransom for many'"?

Our best example of servanthood is Jesus. Look how He relinquished all of His rights to reconcile an entire world. So the next time a Caucasian person asks you a question you may view as ridiculous from your perspective, why not respond lovingly with the answer? I must admit when I was younger I was very annoyed at any inquiries about my culture. Now that I am older and much wiser I view these questions as their interest in who I am and their attempt at reconciliation. *The key ingredient in reconciliation is to love your neighbor as yourself.*

Step #5—Exercise patience and self-control when contending with racism. Try not to attribute occasional strife from our brothers and sisters as always racism. Just like being in a marriage, aggravations and annoyances cannot be avoided when you have two different human beings trying to function as one body. There will be some trials. In a marriage you have to walk in complete forgiveness, with patience and perseverance. So it is when attempting to reconcile with our brothers and sisters.

Don't cry wolf unless one is really chasing you. Perhaps you are not qualified for the employment opportunity. Just maybe someone had a higher offer than you for the house. Maybe the clerk at the department store really wanted to help you. Ask the Lord for wide-open eyes to see when you are being justly denied because of race and the discernment for how to deal with it.

I am sure if I surveyed every African-American individual who is reading this book, they could tell me at least one hundred different situations where they were discriminated unjustly in their lifetime. It was early when I learned my first lesson in racism. I realized at age three I couldn't take a vacation from my heritage. There we were: my mom, dad and I who wanted to take part in an activity most Americans do, eating. My dad being a military man at the time was used to the freedom we experienced as governmental employees.

Apparently I chose a restaurant off base. Just about the time we exited the car and walked into the tiny establishment, we were greeted by two huge, pale white, husky looking men at the door. My mother, who is filled with wisdom, had the discernment to know that men had egos and this could get very ugly. When confronted with where did we think we were going (expletives deleted) she replied, "We just wanted to pick up some food." The men firmly and insensitively pointed to the back of the restaurant and said, "Get back into your car and drive around the back. You'll get your food there." My dad, still operating with his full ego intact, decided he would show them. He was planning to drive off without the food. My mother, who knew my dad extremely well, decided she wouldn't say a word, because usually my dad did the opposite of what she would suggest anyway. She just sat there and prayed.

A few seconds later my dad said, "You know, I was thinking about leaving that food here since they treated us that way. But you know, the greater example to our child would be to take it and allow them to mistreat us. We are the Christians here. Let's model Christ." My mom chimed in, "Sounds like a good idea, and when we get home let's throw the food away." She smiled and thanked the Lord for sparing our lives.

After that experience there are still some places in the United States I don't go. I learned three key lessons from that experience. The first one was when confronted with racism it is best to exercise true humility. I think my dad's response literally saved our lives. The second lesson was we as Christ followers don't have to insist on our rights. When we die to ourselves we give up all rights. Dad could have been dead right (literally) if he had retaliated. The third lesson I extracted from this experience was that my parents both had the ability to exercise self-control and great restraint. They were very patient and had the grace to reason through a potential conflict. Another lesson I learned was when it comes to your family, do whatever it takes to ensure their safety. Use wisdom.

Another means of exercising patience and self-control is to avoid conflict. I don't go anywhere I perceive I am not welcome. You won't see me traveling through any small towns in the south. I remember one occasion when I traveled by bus to Florida my sophomore year at college. The bus pulled into a rest stop for dinner. Being the only African American on board, I asked the Lord for a special dispensation of protection. Although my traveling buddies were very receptive to the ideas espoused by the United States constitution concerning my right to life, liberty and the pursuit of happiness, I perceived that the waitress and customers did not share their sentiment. As I surveyed the greasy spoon diner, I noticed the clientele wasn't quite thrilled with my arrival. I sat with my head bowed low desperately avoiding any eye contact. I asked the Lord again for protection as my companions were totally oblivious to my plight.

Just as I anticipated, the waitress never asked me what I wanted to eat. For the sake of peace I swallowed my pride. As I watched everyone around me eat, my best friend took up an offering of food as the waitress and patrons watched in total disgust. I am not called to be a trailblazer insisting on my own rights. Who cares about laws that entitle me to access anywhere, I don't have anything to prove. I have an identity in Jesus Christ and frankly that is the only one that counts.

Another example of exercising self-control and patience is to see the glass as half full rather than half empty. The more positive outlook you have about life, the more pleasant your experiences will be. So if you are walking the planet with a huge chip on your shoulder and think everyone is out to offend you, you're probably right.

Whenever an issue of racism or discrimination surfaces, take a deep breath and try to analyze it from every angle. Examine the pros and cons of the situation. Try to read between the lines. For example, I was in the hospital waiting room and as soon as I arrived to the counter the first thing the nurse asked me was for my welfare card. As I observed the nurse next to us interacting with her patient I waited calmly to determine whether this was a routine procedure. The other nurse never asked her Caucasian patient for her welfare card. After exhaling and inhaling a few times and asking the Lord for the fruit of the Spirit qualities (all nine of them immediately), I asked the Lord for words, a double-dip dosage of humility and a heaping measure of self-restraint thrown in for good measure, and they came.

"Miss Know-it-all (again, name changed), I am wondering why you asked me for a welfare card. I noticed the other patients were not asked." She replied, "Because your chart has a huge red sticker on it indicating you are a public aid recipient." You see, if I insisted that she was racist and she was assuming one of the stereotypes about us, I would have blown it totally out of proportion. Upon further review of our file she realized she had the wrong folder. After her apology I felt completely exonerated. The way I responded allowed us to get to the heart of the matter without doing any significant damage to either party.

We cannot walk around paranoid and label every mistreatment as racism. We would be doing ourselves a great injustice. What a psychological toll this would create on our own psyche and yet an even greater burden on our Caucasian brothers and sisters. They shouldn't be forced to evaluate every word, deed or action they make while interacting with us. We need to exonerate them from every offense, whether they are unintentional or intentionally made against us. We have to grant them freedom to be who they are and forgive them daily just like Jesus Christ forgave us of our trespasses.

We also need to hold them accountable for their actions if they offend us. Whenever someone makes an offensive joke about my race I don't laugh or pass it off as harmless. I make it extremely clear by my facial expression that I didn't appreciate the comment and later when I am alone with the individual, I will recall it to their attention. Lately in conflicts I have been releasing them to the Lord for retribution. We need to pick our fights carefully and choose our battles wisely.

Keep in mind not every situation is race-related. Perhaps the man who just got in front of you in the grocery store line is in a hurry. Had you been Caucasian I'm sure he would have been just as rude. Let him cut in front of you. Tell him to help himself. Life's too short to get upset about such trivial matters. You have a calling on your life to fulfill. Don't get distracted.

When you think racism is in operation, try to keep some type of balance between resigned acceptance and active confrontation. This is how I decide which battles I will fight. I assess whether the situation is based on perceived stereotypical assumptions about us or just plain ignorance. Since the example of the woman in the clinic was based on stereotypes, I felt it was my civil duty to correct her. The grocery store situation was based strictly on ignorance and I discern there were no hateful motives. For about half of the racist attitudes I am confronted with, I don't give them the time of day. I will point out to the individual that I know what they are trying to do to me, but I don't have enough time to deal with them. I have more important matters to contend with, like trying to further God's kingdom. Besides, nothing will be gained by me acknowledging their racist attitudes. Most racists already know they are.

I am surely not advocating being ignorant of Satan's devices. I am just saying we don't need to set up a tent in the Enemy's camp. Just remember that sometimes our Caucasian brothers and sisters just aren't aware of their offenses. For example, I had a woman recently tell me that all black people could sing very well. So to prove her wrong I broke into a rendition of my favorite Barbara Streisand song, "The Way We Were." After laughing hysterically for about three minutes she recanted her statement. With that little incident I wonder what other stereotypes about us are floating around. I've also experienced in educational settings where, because my son was a little active, that many of the teachers, social workers and principals advised me to place him on medication. On occasion there are children who are hyperactive and need to be medicated. However, that should be done on a case by case basis with a thorough medical examination and not based on a stereotype of black boys. Although racism at times can be quite malignant, there is usually no radiation treatment needed.

The best plan as African Americans when confronting racism is to educate, not hate. Let me give you one more example of stereotypes. I wanted to purchase a new car. I was dressed unusually casual and based on that premise I knew that I was about to be taken for a ride. When I asked to see the latest Mercedes, the salesman said, "Perhaps we need to qualify you first." To which I replied, "Since I am planning to pay in cash, I don't think prequalification would be necessary. But since we need to do extra paperwork, I'll just go to your competitor down the street." With those words he suddenly became very accommodating.

Another way to exercise patience and self-control would be to respond very quickly to racially offensive remarks before they become abusive. I can recall in high school when we were viewing a film one of my classmates made a derogatory remark. A Caucasian man was being arrested for selling drugs. My classmate said something to the effect of why was he being arrested, he committed no crime, the real criminals live in the ghetto and are the ones taking the drugs. I immediately replied, "They are arresting the right person, because if he wasn't selling the drugs none of the people in the ghetto or affluent suburbs would be able to take them."

You would be surprised how much drug trafficking occurs in white suburbia. You would be even more surprised that the soccer mom and the man at the suburban grocery store are probably running a meth lab in their home. We need to educate as much as possible without taking offense.

When seeking to forgive our Caucasian brothers and sisters in Christ, realize that we owe no man any apology for the way a member of our race acts. Just because a small portion of members of our race may be murders, prostitutes or drug addicts doesn't mean they can ascribe these traits to our entire race. No more than we can assign the horrendous acts of the KKK to the entire Caucasoid race. Just remember when we are in their company and one of us acts like we have no sense as a fellow brother or sister, politely disapprove of the behavior and not the individual.

Another one of my pet peeves is we don't support each other economically. If you know a brother or sister with a product just as good or superior as a product of our Caucasian counterparts, why not purchase it from them? We need to support one another even when the cost of it is slightly higher.

Try to remember when we live in the very affluent areas, Caucasians may have very limited exposure to us and often need explanations. Try not to read hostility into their inquisitiveness. I remember the time my daughter's school called and told me they thought she was ill because her skin was very gray. After I explained to them that we have very dry skin and I would send in baby oil for them to administer to her when necessary, they were relieved. What would be the point of me condemning them? Who would that serve?

When confronted with racism, always conduct yourself with class, tact and dignity. Try to be the individual who exemplifies Jesus Christ. If you are stopped by a police officer, be polite. Handle yourself properly. God has placed them in authority whether they deserve it or not. Be nonconfrontational and nonthreatening. Make no uncertain moves. Follow their instructions exactly. Keep your hands where they can see them at all times. Never go into your glove compartment for anything. If your registration is there, ask permission to get it. Never jump out of your vehicle. Proceed very slowly when interacting with the police. If the officer acts erroneously write down his badge number and call his commanding officer later. If enough of us utilize the proper channels we may be able to curtail mistreatment. Let's not contribute to any additional police harassment by talking back.

The "black rage" defense is out of the question for us who are called by Christ. The Bible reveals that Jesus only went into a rage when people were making a mockery out of the temple. And under those circumstances His temper was controlled. The only rage we should be experiencing is rage against the kingdom of darkness. "The kingdom of heaven has been forcefully advancing, and forceful men lay hold of it." (Matthew11:12). We must forbid the devil from stripping away from us the promises of God. We are a blessed people with a rich godly heritage to leave for generations to come. To allow black rage to be used as a defense in the legal system because you didn't exercise self-control and restraint makes you just as guilty as the individual who perpetrated the discrimination. We all know the high cost of frustration, humiliation, depression and aggravation. It costs us our health. Let's not allow Satan to take our lives. We are bought with such a high price.

As Christ followers we have to stay off the defensive road. We need to take the shield away from our hearts and cover it with the breastplate of righteousness. I use to prepare myself psychologically every time I left the house in an attempt to avoid being wounded. It wasn't until I realized that the more I erected a wall around my heart the more isolated I became. Now when I leave the house I encourage myself in the Lord by speaking spiritual songs. When people ask me how I am, I respond "I am blessed and highly favored." And you wouldn't be surprised by the petitions granted on my behalf when I interact cross-culturally. Whenever you are tempted to build a barrier between you and another individual, remember to march around that wall until it falls down.

Rely on your family to provide a safe haven for you from the world. Family members have a way of helping us to deflect some of racism's stings. Our heritage has strong kinship ties that we inherited from our ancestors who were very tribal. We have a tendency to depend on our family. We are known for taking one another in. So allow our nuclear and extended family members to comfort us and to be vessels of mercy and grace in our times of need. If you are not a regular church attendee, you need to become one. The church for many years has been our refuge. It's the only institution in our community that has remained constant all of these years since slavery. That worship service on Sunday morning for the slaves was the only time the masters didn't monitor their every move. Even today the church remains a social structure that serves as a forum for ministering to our needs.

Try to exercise as much self-control as humanly possible, and then ask the Lord for an extra measure. If we retaliate, don't we become worse than our transgressor? Racism is no reflection on who you are. After all, you didn't create yourself, now did you?

In racially reconciling, exert all energy into becoming all you can be. Try not to dwell on the negative. Focus on your uniqueness, intellectual skills, wisdom and your strengths. There is no one on earth like us. We are fearfully and wonderfully made. So choose joy. Laugh more and stand on the promises of God.

Step #6 — Support your fellow African-American brothers and sisters who choose to reconcile. I can recall numerous times I was literally persecuted because I attend a predominately Caucasian church. There were occasions when I would walk into a church and if I didn't see at least twenty African-American people I would leave, never to return. But if you leave because you don't see anyone who resembles you, you are wrong and the devil has just set you up. I remember during one of our services the devil was telling me, "You cannot stay here. It's too white." I was just about convinced and out the door again when the pastor stood up and said, "There is someone here who is planning to leave because they don't see diversity here. That is a trick of the enemy. Don't fall for it."

When racing towards reconciliation, if we are concerned about what other people think, we might as well leave the fuel tank on empty because we are going nowhere quickly. If I allowed my family and friends to influence me, I would still be in my old black church sitting quietly in the back pew staying in my place. It was the white church that recognized I had gifts, talents, and an anointing, who welcomed me with wide-open hearts to join them in ministry. It was there I accepted my call to pastor God's people.

Please don't refer to me as an Uncle Tom, Oreo or a sellout, or whatever derogatory remarks you may create. These thoughts are very harmful and remind me of the time when there were yard servants and house servants during slavery. It was almost like there was a class system between both sets of slaves. How ridiculous it was when one group of indentured servants would tell on the other group when they both are enslaved. Let's grow up. Let's use wisdom. It matters what journey we take to heaven. So please don't call me out of my name. I am a child of God endeavoring to live a life worthy of His calling. Besides, if none of us joins a predominately white church, how are we going to integrate it?

Step #7—Join organizations that are in the process of trying to reconcile cross-culturally. We need to join churches and organizations like Promise Keepers who have been very intentional in trying to reconcile across the color lines. Try not to start your own organization. Join an existing one. If we begin too many ministry models similar to those already standing, we may fail by going it alone and defeat the purpose of integration.

Step #8—Assist in dispelling stereotypes. Many prejudices are birthed out of ignorance. Sometimes individuals turn the television on and see an African American committing a violent crime and may ascribe that behavior to everyone in our race. Or they may see someone on public transportation who is yelling obscenities and assign that character trait to all African Americans. I can recall a Caucasian couple telling me that in the school where they work, which is predominately African American, all the children do is swear. Without hesitation I chimed in, "That's quite an interesting assumption because the school my children attend, which happens to be a predominately Caucasian parochial school...you should hear some of the language coming from those children. And I know at least five African-American children who never swear at all." They didn't know how to respond.

We as Christ followers should dispel such stereotypes and take offense when someone participates in indecent behavior. Personally when I am in public and someone is using foul language, I bring it to their attention by saying, "You know, I would really appreciate it if you could refrain from using that type of language around me. Thank you."

We must also eliminate the stereotype that we are all lazy and lack professionalism when it comes to our employment. When searching for employment, make sure you are the most qualified educationally and have the appropriate job skills. Once you are employed come in before everyone arrives and leave after everyone departs. Make coffee even though it's not in your job description. Most importantly, dress for success. Formulate a plan of action that will communicate you are the best employee that company ever hired.

Don't engage in employee gossip. Never tell your personal business. It may come back to haunt you one day. Do your forty hours and leave. Don't make personal calls, and complete all assigned tasks or ask for extensions if necessary. Keep pursuing your goals. Move full steam ahead. Press towards the mark. You are working for the Lord and He will reward you for your diligence. When His favor is on you, no one on earth can do you harm. You will eat the fruit of the land because you are obeying God.

In cases of overt racism, of course you need to speak up. I remember being asked by a company to change my hairstyle. I had a manager tell me, "You need to look more mainstream." When I inquired as to what mainstream was he replied, "Just observe your coworkers." When I looked around and saw nothing but white coworkers, I asked him if a judge in a civil suit would agree with his mainstream statement, and of course he conceded and I wore my braids. Recognize racism, deal with it professionally, in stride, while continuing to pursue your calling.

In the educational system, if there is ever any question as to whether you received an inaccurate grade, instead of always making accusations that it's racism, how about reasoning with the professor? Ask for an appointment and calmly inquire into how you could improve your grade. Usually when gently approaching someone, they will have a greater tendency to want to resolve the conflict. Any accusations or belligerent behavior only seeks to alienate your adversary even further. The art of negotiation will help you to win that person over to your side.

In certain circumstances there may be complete personality clashes that are not racially motivated. There were times when a professor simply didn't like me because of who I was. It had nothing to do with my skin color. He may have been intimidated by my aggressive, strong-willed and confident personality. Despite all attempts at pouring my heart, mind and soul into my course work, I still only made it out of there with a miserable C. It wasn't until I entered graduate school and submitted the same paper where I earned an A that it reinforced what I originally knew. There just wasn't any chemistry.

Not every war is worth the battle. Pick and choose your fights. The C grade was not life altering. It didn't affect my grade point average in the least. If we entertained all the negative situations in our life we would never have any time for ministry.

Now sometimes we may be called by God for a greater good to litigate on the behalf of African Americans who are to follow us. I cannot help but think about the consequences of Rosa Park's actions. An entire civil rights movement may have been averted if it was not for her stand. Or how about my girlfriend, Valerie Bennett, who took on an entire school system and won. Valerie paved the way for African Americans and other minorities to be hired in our local school district.

Whenever the Lord tells us to effect change for a greater cause, you will receive specific instructions and a great anointing to complete the task. No one can keep you from your destiny in the Lord when you are called according to His purposes.

Step #9 — Promote your identity in Christ, not in your race. If we are truly in Jesus Christ our identity should be in Him only. The black power movement is an ideology we must refrain from embracing. I understand the significant role this movement had in the early sixties. It was designed to give us self-esteem and provide unity amongst us. However, when we place our culture before the Lord we begin to worship who we are and not Whose we are.

When we become intentional in bonding all races together, and acknowledging the masterful work of an Omnipotent Creator, we will understand our purposes for living. Celebrate who you are as a person in Jesus Christ because the Lord delights in our appreciation of who He created us to be.

To promote and favor your race over others is very destructive and perpetuates the same racial discrimination we are trying to avoid. There is something distorted about us attending a predominantly African-American church one hour away when there may be a Bible-teaching Caucasian church a block away from our home. Try visiting that church and attend services enough times to assess whether God has called you there.

Step #10 — Live out your faith in Jesus. We have to extend mercy whenever our Caucasian sisters and brothers attempt to reconcile. We cannot question every act or motive. It takes both parties to reconcile. When in question about their sincerity, always err on the side of grace.

In order for us to fully participate in reconciliation we have to possess a living, vibrant and active faith in Jesus Christ. Only with an anointing and the indwelling power of the Holy Spirit will we be able to achieve racial harmony. It requires a tremendous amount of patience. We will be stretched beyond measure and be very uncomfortable. We will discover gifts and talents we were unaware we had. We will be supernaturally revived in our attempts to race towards reconciliation. So get ready!

Chapter Eight

Interracial and Adoptive Families Only!

This is a subject very dear to my heart. I am also an adoptive mother. Although our home is not an interracial one I still identify with you. I am raising children with special needs and we are facing similar challenges you face from day to day. Discrimination still exists for us. It is simply in a different form.

First of all I would like to esteem you highly for such a self-sacrificial commitment you have made to our Lord. You are a true blessing. The Lord is quite pleased with your actions. You will undoubtcdly facc racism and discrimination simply bccausc of your children. Your life will be tremendously altered. There may be places inaccessible to you because of your children. There may be invitations you will not receive. Teachers you may have to educate. Christians (yes Christians!) who may discourage your endeavors before the children even arrive. There may be family members who will disavow any knowledge of ever being related to you. There may be employers who may overlook you during promotion timc. Thcrc may even be pastors who will forget to address your unique concerns from their pulpits.

Sorry about the grim picture. It doesn't look too promising, does it? But contrary to popular opinion, in Christ all things are possible. So how would you like for me to encourage you since I have given you such a grim prognosis?

We have hope in Jesus Christ. And hopefully you've read the other chapters of this book first (or do you survey the table of contents and pick out the chapters that apply to you and read them first like I do?) Well, in any case let's begin with a story about an interracial marriage.

If you are an interracial couple who knows that God ordained your marital covenant, you are in great company with Moses and his wife Zipporah. They had one of the earliest recorded cross-cultural marriages. Let's take a quick look at their story.

According to Numbers 12:1-16, "Miriam and Aaron began to talk against Moses because of his Cushite wife, for he had married a Cushite. 'Has the Lord spoken only through Moses?' they asked. 'Hasn't he also spoken through us?' And the Lord heard this. (Now Moses was a very humble man, more humble than anyone else on the face of the earth.) At once the Lord said to Moses, Aaron and Miriam, 'Come out to the Tent of Meeting, all three of you.' So the three of them came out. Then the Lord came down in a pillar of cloud; he stood at the entrance to the Tent and summoned Aaron and Miriam. When both of them stepped forward, he said, 'Listen to my words: "When a prophet of the Lord is among you, I reveal myself to him in visions, I speak to him in dreams. But this is not true of my servant Moses; he is faithful in all my house. With him I speak face to face, clearly and not in riddles; he sees the form of the Lord. Why then were you not afraid to speak against my servant Moses?"'

The anger of the Lord burned against them, and he left them. When the cloud lifted from above the Tent, there stood Miriam—leprous, like snow. Aaron turned toward her and saw that she had leprosy; and he said to Moses, 'Please, my Lord, do not hold against us the sin we have so foolishly committed. Do not let her be like a stillborn infant coming from its mother's womb with its flesh half eaten away.' So Moses cried out to the Lord, 'O God, please heal her!' The Lord replied to Moses, 'If her father had spit in her face, would she not have been in disgrace for seven days? Confine her outside the camp for seven days; after that she can be brought back.' So Miriam was confined outside the camp for seven days, and the people did not move on till she was brought back. After that, the people left Hazeroth and encamped in the Desert of Paran."

In verse 1 we see Miriam and Aaron, who were gossiping about their brother's wife. That was their first mistake. One should never slander another human being, especially a prophet of God. When you speak ill of them you are actually mocking their Creator. Proverbs 18:21 states, "The tongue has the power of life and death, and those who love it will eat its fruit." This verse communicates that the tongue can be a deadly weapon. When misused it can cut like a two-edged sword. In reconciling we should bridle our tongue by allowing no harsh words against anyone to escape. There is something wrong when a Christ follower assassinates a fellow believer's character by speaking harsh words against them. We should concentrate on esteeming others higher than ourselves.

In reconciling cross-culturally this problem is at the heart of racism. Not only are we destroying a man's reputation when we make derogatory statements, we are also betraying the Lord whose second greatest commandment is to love your neighbor as yourself.

As an interracial couple, you have likely been faced with your share of criticism. If God called you together to be in covenant relationship for a lifetime, let no man separate you. You owe no man any apologies or explanations regarding your choice of a mate. In fact, don't even waste your precious time elaborating on God's instructions for you and your spouse. I have very close friends who, when they announced their engagement, were bombarded by statements like, "What about your children?" "Will you raise them black or white?" "God didn't mean for the races to intermingle." "What about what the Bible says about being unequally yoked?" "Have you ever been to a twenty-fifth wedding anniversary of an interracial couple?"(Frankly, I can't recall attending a twenty-fifth wedding anniversary celebration of a Caucasian couple recently.) This couple felt like they were committing a cardinal sin by marrying each other.

If you are in need of some positive reinforcement concerning your interracial marriage, you're in good company with Moses who married a Cushite woman. In verse 1 we see that Aaron and Miriam's opposition against his marriage to Zipporah was based on the law that prohibited intermarriage between Israelites and foreigners. Deuteronomy 7:3-4 states, "Do not intermarry with them. Do not give your daughters to their sons...for they will turn your sons away from following me to serve other gods, and the Lord's anger will burn against you and will quickly destroy you."

In Numbers 25 we see the devastating effects foreign women had on Israelite men and how a plague destroyed them. And Ezra chapters 9 to 10 recalls a time when all foreign wives were returned to their original homes. Therefore Miriam and Aaron thought they were justified in complaining to Moses. After all, the law supported their claim.

In verse 2 we witness their challenge to Moses's authority. They argue that they have a voice from the Lord also. They are quite adamant about Moses's violation of tradition.

In reconciling you will have those voices that want to stick to tradition. They will embrace a philosophy that communicates the old ways are the best way. There will be those in leadership who have done something a certain way for one hundred years and are not willing to compromise. Because their great, great, great-grandfather did something a certain way they have to continue. There is a church in my local community that has officially died because the leadership is not willing to give up the pulpit because he has been the pastor for over forty years. All the members have virtually left the church. It is quite sad when a pastor thinks he is indispensable, wanting to hold on to traditions and allows a vibrant church to literally die.

Another issue you may face in reconciliation is people will challenge your credibility. I have yet to speak at a conference where I have not been challenged in this area. I learned early in my speaking career that an impressive biography is not necessary. My biographies only include the title of my position, references to my children, and what activities I enjoy in my spare time. Consequently, when I begin speaking the audience generally thinks I am not credible, and I am usually asked profound questions at the end of the session. For the most part I am able to answer these questions. Occasionally, when it's a difficult one, I will try to answer it for them at a later time after I have researched the correct answer.

Whenever you begin teaching or leading a small group, you don't have to be an expert on the topic of racial reconciliation. Nor do you have to be concerned about your credentials. As long as you are called and have a heart after God concerning reconciliation, you are qualified. Have an attitude that communicates to everyone that you can do all things through Christ. Embrace a humility that allows God to do a mighty work in you. Be a willing vessel.

In verse 3 we witness the humility of Moses. He was devout in righteousness. His meekness was an attribute that gave him a higher status than any other man of his day. His charisma and leadership qualities were two of God's greatest gifts to him.

In verse 4 the Lord stepped in. He came to the defense of his humble servant. He told Aaron and Miriam how favored Moses was because He spoke with him face to face. Moses had some serious clout with the Lord. He was greater than the prophets before him.

When you are called to go forth in reconciling cross-culturally, don't operate in fear or hesitation. The Lord has your back. You are favored whenever you are operating out of your comfort zone. The Lord gives you a special anointing and dispensation of grace to run this race. So step out in faith and "trust in the Lord with all your heart and lean not on your own understanding; in all your ways acknowledge him, and he will make your paths straight" (Proverbs3:5).

In verse 9 we see the Lord's anger. By this time I wonder if our friends Miriam and Aaron were shaking in their sandals. I know I would be. In fact, if I were them, when the Lord first appeared in the pillar of cloud I would have immediately dropped to my knees and said, "Lord, there's not a problem here. We've worked through everything, and would you forgive me? I am back now and everything is okay."

I would have also asked the Lord to stay around a little longer, because as soon as He disappears we are in huge trouble, the same with reconciliation. You always want the Lord to be around you in your attempts. You cannot accomplish any tasks without Him. So always be in good standing with your spouse, children, family members, church leadership and with the Lord, because you will definitely need them.

In verse 10 we witness the wrath of God on them immediately. I guess Miriam hadn't read the Old Testament yet to realize that God has another side. She was ignorant. In racial reconciliation we cannot afford to be ignorant. It is not bliss in this situation. We must be aware of the consequences of not being informed. "Do your best to present yourself to God as one approved, a workman who does not need to be ashamed and who correctly handles the word of truth" (2 Timothy 2:15).

This act of God demonstrated to everyone that Moses was a real man of God. In verse 11, after witnessing the wrath of God, Aaron became an instant believer. He cried out in defense of his sister for Moses not to hold that sin against Miriam. We as believers usually repent whenever there is an immediate consequence.

In verse 13 Moses's humility convicts him to immediately intercede on Miriam's behalf. Moses calls forth God's healing power. He's already aware of His ability to heal since he has already experienced it with the Israelites.

In racing towards reconciliation you will need to intercede on the behalf of the people you are attempting to reconcile with. At times they will be oblivious to your mission statement. Nevertheless you are still required by God to press on in all your attempts. There will be times when they will annoy you because their values contradict yours. For example, I was asked to volunteer working with single mothers for a year. I was so excited about the opportunity. But after six weeks of dealing with these young women I was completely burned out. They had so many issues that I felt totally inadequate to deal with them. Although I was committed to these women it was only daily intercession that kept me going. There were times I wanted to run out the front door. Their morality was so different than mine. They didn't think anything of having babies out of wedlock year after year. They lacked any motivation and allowed their boyfriends to mercilessly physically and emotionally abuse them. I literally felt like I had been run over by a bulldozer when our sessions were over. After a one-year commitment, I released myself from that calling because my passion to work with them waned.

In verse 14 the Lord told Moses, listen, girlfriend messed up big time. There is no need for you to contest this; I am trying to prove a point. She not only sinned against you, Moses, but she sinned against me. And frankly, I am not tolerating this. So Miriam had to pay for her sins.

Whenever there is sin in our lives I will guarantee you it won't go unpunished. You may get away with it for the moment, but trust me on this one—the Lord sees it and there will be consequences to pay even if you repent. God publicly rebuked her and demanded she face public humiliation. She was banished from the camp for seven days. And the people did not move until she was allowed to return. I wonder if Miriam ever repented. There is no indication in the Bible that she repented. The healing came from Aaron and Moses's intercession.

The moral of this story is we need to be careful how we treat a prophet of God. There are tremendous consequences when we mistreat God's elect. As an interracial couple, take heart in knowing that you are an earthly example of how heaven's going to look. From Acts 17:26 we know that, "From one man he made every nation of men, that they should inhabit the whole earth; and he determined the times set for them and the exact places where they should live." This means that people from all tongues, nations and tribes will be sitting together at the feet of Jesus. So you need to start preparing your heart for this.

As an interracial couple you will inevitably be confronted with hate or bigotry regarding your marital choice. In this event take the high road when dealing with ignorance. Don't ever involve yourself with heated debates. It's not anyone else's concern. The covenant is between you two and the Lord.

When seeking to reconcile interracially in your own family, here's a list of ten suggestions.

1. **Give your children an identity in Jesus Christ first.** The first order of business is to give your children a godly heritage. Once you have rooted and grounded them in who they are as God's child, you can begin assisting them with learning about their culture. *We waste a lot of time trying to cure racism. Instead we should try to prevent the illness through multicultural education.* Be proactive in teaching them about their rich heritage when they are old enough to comprehend. Be intentional in making them aware of their history. This can be done by reading books and attending special programs in the community geared towards celebrating black history. During February there are endless resources in the newspaper of events scheduled throughout the month. Also be willing to drop by your children's school and see what type of curriculum they are offering that reinforces your children's racial identity. In February I would call all of my children's schools to ask permission to present a dramatic production of black history. It gave me an opportunity to introduce Jesus to the children in the public school setting. Instilling positive self-esteem in your child is one of the most powerful weapons for combating racism. If you teach your child that he or she is the cutest, smartest, wittiest, and the best thing that ever happen to humanity, you are off to a great start. You have to ingrain in them that they can do all things through Christ and nothing is impossible.

2. **Revaluate relationships with families and friends that are not life-sustaining.** In our attempts to give our children healthy self-esteem we may have to clean our closets of dysfunctional people in our lives. We may have to tell our friends and family members that we are taking a sabbatical from our relationships with them during our child-rearing years. For example, when I adopted my special needs children, I literally terminated several friendships from individuals who did not affirm my children. I had to let them go. I was working for the Lord. I didn't have time to sit around and debate whether or not I was fit enough to sustain all the challenges of raising special needs children. Besides, the Lord didn't tell me to ask for their approval. Be aware of people who tell you that the Lord gave them an instruction about your life. Make sure you are in right relationship with Him so you will have direct access to the Lord if He wants to tell you something concerning your life. We must also protect our children from good intentions of well-meaning people. In this culture there is a tendency to favor children based on their physical appearance and personality. I cannot begin to warn you about the horror stories I've overcome of people favoring one of my children over the others. You must consistently be aware of people who will seek to alienate your children from each other based on the complexion of their skin. Guard against people who favor interracially mixed children over your African-American children because of their unique features. How devastating that can be to a child's self-image. The Lord has placed us in charge over their souls and we will be held accountable for our actions. So be aware and use discernment.

3. **Surround yourself with African-American friends.** It is vital that if you do not have any African-American friends in your lives that you run out and find some immediately. It is imperative that African-American children have positive role models that look just like them to assist them with forming a healthy identity and good self-esteem. Ask local black churches to give you a list of older African Americans who could serve as surrogate grandparents. There are also Christian social service agencies that can assist you with finding positive role models.

4. **Join or attend a racially diverse church.** Given your circumstances this may not be very practical if you are called to a specific church. If the church God called you to is not racially diverse, it is your responsibility to provide a supplement. This could be attained by visiting other churches or finding another setting such as an Awanas or vacation Bible school in order for your children to have that need met. I grew up in an African-American church even though I lived in a predominately white community so church was not an issue for me. But once I had children I changed my church affiliation to a church that was predominantly white. So in order to enhance my children's exposure to our culture, they attended a Boy Scouts program, vacation Bible school, camps and any other activities I could find in our black community to create a balance for them.

5. **Serve ethnically diverse foods.** Introduce your children to foods associated with their culture. If you don't know where to start, ask your new African-American friends if they could teach you how to cook. There are also numerous cookbooks on the subject in local bookstores. Maybe for the next birthday you can plan a potluck and invite everyone to prepare a family dish that represents their heritage. If you are not passionate about cooking there are several soul food restaurants located in major cities that can prepare this type of food for you and perhaps deliver it to you in time for your dinner tonight.

6. **Have discussions about the news media and their distorted images of African Americans.** If you tune in to television and there are negative images of African Americans you need to make sure that you explain this problem to your children. You may also have to tune out some television programs that portray African Americans in stereotypical fashion. My children's television viewing is very limited. They are not allowed to watch any network or cable television unless I am in the room to filter out the garbage. Those cable networks that show music videos of African Americans dancing and singing are particularly repulsive to me and do not represent our culture accurately at all. You will especially have to monitor their musical taste when they are older as well. We have a rule in my house that if it doesn't glorify God in any way, it's in the trash.

7. **Attend culturally stimulating events.** Make sure your children receive well-rounded exposure to culturally stimulating events. Don't take your child to a rap concert because they express a desire for that. Why not take them to see the Boys Choir of Harlem sing or Kathleen Battle? Try not to reinforce stereotypes about us in your own behavior. Teach your children how to be unique. Support their varied interests. For years I never knew my sons liked the sport of volleyball until one day they came home and said

they made the team. Now what if I had discouraged them based on the fact I've never seen an African-American volleyball player, that would have done them a tremendous disservice, now wouldn't it? Not only was I caught off guard by that experience, but I also have a son who is an avid chess player. What if I had encouraged him to pursue basketball or baseball instead of chess? We would be squelching his God-given talents. And he wouldn't have earned fourth place in the state of Illinois in 2003.

8. **Encourage open dialogue about any topic.** The key to raising African-American children with healthy self-images is to listen attentively to all their concerns. Try to relate to their perspective at all times. Racism will not be evident to children because they are generally color blind. So try to negotiate on their behalf using wisdom and discernment. There will be times when you will have to gather the facts and you will need to be prepared to make an unfavorable decision against your child. I can say out of the very few conflicts I've had from other people regarding my children, my children were usually wrong and misinterpreted the other individuals' actions. After hearing all of the information and praying, I was able to make a wise decision that benefited all parties involved. With African-American children growing up in a predominately white society, there will be issues of discrimination that you may not possibly understand from your perspective. If that ever occurs, it would be advisable for you to seek out an African-American friend who could be a sounding board and shed light on the issue. When you parent cross-culturally you have to be very resourceful and take on the attitude of the African proverb, "It takes an entire village to raise a child."

9. **Support your child's desire for same-culture friends without compromising your moral standards.** There is nothing wrong with your child seeking wholesome relationships with people of his own heritage. The only time it becomes a problem is if his friendships are detrimental to his moral development. We must be actively involved in our children's lives. As parents we are never to compromise our Christian values for the sake of attaining racial harmony. For example, when my teenage sons began group dating, I would literally ask them to make me a list of all the children they were going to be involved with. I didn't care what their complexions were. If they were not people of integrity with moral virtue, my sons could not interact with them. Remember the Scripture verse 1 Corinthians 15:33, "'Bad company corrupts good character.'" After they compiled the list, I would ask them whether this individual had the same values as our family, and if they didn't, they had to choose another friend to hang out with.

10. **Model reconciliation for your children.** Make sure you set a good example of reconciliation. They are watching you very carefully. Be honest in all actions. Watch every word that proceeds out of your mouth. If your attitude is negative towards some African Americans, you are automatically indicting your child since that is their heritage.

Raising African-American children in a Caucasian family isn't that difficult. It just requires a little more intentionally in exposing them to their culture, which is what we all should be doing anyway.

Chapter Nine

Reparations or Seventy-seven Times?

Is there a more controversial subject than the discussion of whether reparations should be paid to African Americans? What is your opinion on this very heated subject? From your Caucasian perspective, do you feel we should be compensated for the trouble we received during slavery?

From my perspective, I strongly disagree with any compensation being paid to any group of people for their mistreatment. I am aware of the reparations paid to other groups during the course of history. However, when we set an amount, who will determine how much money each individual receives? What is the dollar amount on an individual being stolen in the middle of the night from their homeland, wrangled up, chained and thrown into a dark slave ship like a caged animal? I've seen animals treated with more dignity. How can we allocate funds for slave owners sexually violating our daughters, wives, aunts, mothers and grandmothers with no fear of consequences and no moral conscience? To have my sister give birth to the slave owner's child and have that baby snatched from her arms... you can compensate us for that? How much is it worth to witness a runaway slave, after their capture, have their foot cut off? How will you compensate us based on the beatings and bruises we received? There is absolutely no amount of money that can be repaid for the atrocities committed against my forefathers.

So for this purpose I will focus on seventy-seven times because, frankly, healing can only occur in the context of redemption. According to Matthew 18:21-22, "Then Peter came to Jesus and asked, 'Lord, how many times shall I forgive my brother when he sins against me? Up to seven times?' Jesus answered, 'I tell you, not seven times, but seventy-seven times.'

Jesus again tells an eloquent parable about an unmerciful servant. The point of the entire story was to highlight what it means to forgive. The story, according to Matthew 18:23-35, captures for its readers a lesson about a king who wanted to settle an account with one of his servants. "As he began the settlement, a man who owed him ten thousand talents was brought to him. Since he was not able to pay, the master ordered that he and his wife and his children and all that he had be sold to repay the debt. The servant fell on his knees before him. "Be patient with me," he begged, "and I will pay back everything." The servant's master took pity on him, canceled the debt and let him go. But when that servant went out, he found one of his fellow servants who owed him a hundred denarii. He grabbed him and began to choke him. "Pay back what you owe me!" he demanded. His fellow servant fell to his knees and begged him, "Be patient with me, and I will pay you back." But he refused. Instead, he went off and had the man thrown into prison until he could pay the debt. When the other servants saw what had happened, they were greatly distressed and went and told their master everything that happened. Then the master called the servant in. "You wicked servant," he said, "I canceled all that debt of yours because you begged me to. Shouldn't you have had mercy on your fellow servant just as I had on you?" In anger his master turned him over to the jailers to be tortured, until he should pay back all he owed. This is how my heavenly Father will treat each of you unless you forgive your brother from your heart.'"

This debt was a result of mismanagement of funds. The debt was not payable because it was so large. This was a hopeless situation, and no matter how much time was allowed to repay, it would be virtually impossible.

In racial reconciliation the debt owed to African Americans is similar to the debt of this servant. It is overwhelmingly colossal to pay back. You could never compensate another human being for loss of self-worth and dignity. So to even suggest that reparations should be given to us is an affront to who we are. The only comfort we seek is mercy from our Lord.

In the Matthew 18 story we see that since the servant could not repay his master he got the bright idea to ask for mercy. What did he have to lose by simply asking for forgiveness? Absolutely nothing and neither do you if you are brave enough to step out on faith. The king was merciful and favorably responded with compassion.

In this story the king symbolized who God is, and the debt is symbolic of sin. The first servant's debt was too large to repay. While the second servant's debt represented a lesser amount, it seemed more logical that the first servant would have forgiven immediately since he was forgiven for such a larger amount. The same holds true for reconciling cross-culturally. We are all sinners saved by grace, so how can we expect to be forgiven if we don't forgive others? When we fail to forgive our brothers and sisters who have done wrong against us, how can we expect God to forgive us?

Forgiveness is a matter of the will, a choice we have to consciously make. It is an intentional act of saying to the offender, "I release you from the offense. And as I choose to release you, I will align my emotions with my heart." When we forgive we release the offender from the power to control our emotions. We become committed to making sure that the offender is restored into a proper relationship.

For African Americans forgiveness involves waiting patiently, gracefully and in a nonconfrontational manner. While waiting for a change to occur remember we have to express Christlike behavior at all times. Those of us called by Christ cannot afford to allow another human being to have that much power over us. Their evil devices cannot take up residence in our hearts or minds unless they are making a mortgage payment. We have to accept contrite apologies and reaffirm our Caucasian brothers and sisters again in love and restore them to their rightful place.

We must be patient, committed and flexible. We have to keep all the lines of communication open and resist the urge to judge their motives. Only the Lord knows the motives of men's hearts and He will judge us accordingly.

I am not advocating that meekness is weakness. I'm just saying to choose your battles wisely because sometimes the war is not worth the effort. Oftentimes we waste so much invaluable time pursuing injustices that we are hindered from fulfilling God's calling.

One of the operating forces of offense is tied into our pride. If we deflate our egos we will have a better response to mistreatment. I would say nine times out of ten we can trace being offended to our inflated view of who we think we are. That is one of the reasons God hates pride. He knows how destructive it can be in our lives.

Just think back a few moments to the last time you were angry at someone. Can you honestly admit that your anger was not motivated by pride? If you said no, you just proved that you are proud. If you said yes, continue reading and I will give you an example of anger motivated by pride.

Remember earlier when I was telling you about my daughter's school calling and telling me that our family would be candidates for receiving financial assistance from local churches at Christmastime? The appropriate response for me should have been no, thank you. Instead I entertained my ego and was tempted to give her full details about how prosperous we were. I wanted her to know that we would send a donation instead of being the recipients of one. My pride forced me to become offended at what she thought would make my day. I did not have to go there with her. All I needed to say was no, thank you and allow her to draw her own conclusions about my refusal. I should not have volunteered what the left hand was doing. If I wanted to make a donation, that should have been between me and the Lord. In allowing my pride to rule the situation I was the one needing to repent after the telephone conversation.

We need to keep our egos in check as African Americans. After all, we are the ones with the hypertension and other diseases characteristic of our culture because of the offenses we allow others to perpetrate against us, many of which could be alleviated if we humbled ourselves.

Humility is a key ingredient to reconciliation. We cannot expect the Holy Spirit to assist us if we don't humble ourselves in the sight of God. We need to realize that we are weak, frail, and incompetent human beings without the Holy Spirit fully operating in us. We have to carefully esteem others higher than ourselves. Their total good and interests should be our highest priority.

Caucasians should never take it personally when an African American releases stored-up hostility. We have been conditioned by our parents to accept mistreatment since the days of slavery. But sometimes you reach the boiling point and it starts to overflow. There may be one time that you will receive the brunt of several hundred years of antagonism in the form of hostility and frustration from an African American you are trying to reconcile with. So if this occurs please don't be offended. Just try again with someone else. And by all means, if you have to stand alone to defend your convictions, stand alone!

To completely forgive we must not ever hold the trespass against the offender. How many of us have heard someone say, "I may forgive that person but I surely will never forget what they've done to me." I strongly disagree with this statement. I think to truly forgive we must forget because if we don't forget, we still have the ability to harbor resentment upon remembrance of the offense. To truly forget is to release from your consciousness the ill deed. For African Americans to forgive slavery and not forget the inhumane acts committed against our forefathers is a higher form of enslavement. We will still be in bondage if we remember what was done to us.

The next time your spouse or someone you are in covenant with offends you, try this exercise. Immediately tell them that "although you have offended me by what you just said to me, I choose not to charge this to your account. I will credit your statement because I am trying to glorify the Lord in all I do. Please allow me to ask you for forgiveness for the sins I have committed against you." Do you see the difference in this response? It is a proactive communication that I have sinned against you instead of if I have sinned against you. After you confess, immediately replace the offense with a pleasant memory you have with that individual and focus your energy on that vision.

Sometimes we will be offended by an individual who will have absolutely no concept of what their offense is. It is our Christian duty to make them aware in a godly manner. We are to speak the truth in love. Perhaps the incident was simply miscommunication. I've had a few of these instances in my life. The most recent example was a lack of communication regarding some expectations. This occurs daily in marriages. In a marital situation each individual brings to the relationship a list of their own expectations of the other spouse. Somehow if these expectations are not clearly communicated prior to the ceremony, the couple will be in for a huge surprise. For example, if you never talked about the woman staying home with the children prior to marriage and all of a sudden she is pregnant and expecting to terminate her employment and you would rather hire a nanny, how many of us know you are headed for some heated debate?

The same with racial reconciliation, if our goals are not clearly communicated, one of the individuals may expect something that is foreign to the other individual. I'll never forget the time I was asked to teach from Proverbs 31. In obedience I prepared a ten-page exegesis of the virtuous woman. Well, by the time my plane landed and I was met at the airport, the program was altered. They decided to change the topic to an unrelated subject, talking about expectations not being clearly communicated. I had to regroup and rely entirely on the leading of the Holy Spirit. And like 2 Timothy 4:2 states, "Preach the Word; be prepared in season and out of season; correct, rebuke and encourage—with great patience and careful instruction." And the Holy Spirit, as always, came through.

We also need to exercise what Colossians 3:13-14 states. "Bear with each other and forgive whatever grievances you may have against one another. Forgive as the Lord forgave you. And over all these virtues put on love, which binds them all together in perfect unity." This verse clearly communicates the importance of love in binding us together in unity. Love is the key ingredient here. We will never be able to forgive if we do it out of a sense of duty or obligation. Our desire to forgive must be motivated by the love we have for another individual.

Another key ingredient to forgiveness is we must learn how to forgive ourselves. Many of us have survived painful and abusive experiences. And although the Lord has forgiven us we still relive and internalize this resentment. Even if you are responsible for your mistreatment from others based on your irresponsible behavior or lack of accountability, you still need to forgive yourself. How can you ever expect someone to forgive you if you haven't started with yourself? It's just not possible. When we walk in complete forgiveness of what we've done to ourselves and others, we give the Lord permission to radically change us and do a work in us we could never comprehend. So release the Lord to change you.

The goal of forgiveness is to have honest and open conversations about our issues. If you make a concerted effort to become acquainted with people different from you, you will be aware of their problems and at least have their perspective. Forgiveness is the ability to discern the multiplicity of challenges and situations associated with your adversity while simultaneously remaining objective. It also involves realizing that just because it wasn't your experience doesn't mean it didn't occur. We all have our own perspective, and it is usually based on our own perceptions.

We have to serve one another. We need to wash our brothers' and sisters' feet like Jesus did. Caucasian followers of Christ, in reconciling, you may have to ask the hard questions:

1. **Can you help me understand your problems from your perspective?**
2. **What can we do to help solve your problems?**
3. **How was your issue resolved in the past?**
4. **What are the solutions you can offer us?**
5. **How can we serve you?**

And the same for us African-American Christ followers. You may have to ask the hard questions also.

1. **How can I open up the lines of communication?**
2. **How can I state my problem without further alienating my Caucasian brother or sister?**
3. **What strongholds will I have to release to spark candid dialogue?**
4. **What are our greatest needs from Caucasians?**
5. **How can we serve our Caucasian brothers and sisters?**

The art of forgiveness can be summed up in the Scripture verse Luke 23:34, "'Father, forgive them, for they do not know what they are doing.'" Just like Jesus as He murmured those final words, we can say the same for those who offend us. We need to ask our heavenly Father to forgive them because of their lack of awareness. We need to advocate on their behalf in humility because the same grace we extend to our fellowman is the same mercy that God will extend to us.

So now that you have mastered forgiveness, let's take a few minutes and recall a brother or sister that you have something against right now. According to Matthew 5:23-24, "'Therefore, if you are offering your gift at the altar and there remember that your brother has something against you, leave your gift there in front of the altar. First go and be reconciled to your brother; then come and offer your gift.'"

So that's the plan, because we will be hindered in reconciling cross-culturally if we don't start with the person we are currently in conflict with. This also includes our spouses. If we cannot walk in full, whole-hearted devotion with our husband or wife, we might as well forget reconciling with anyone else. The Lord cannot honor a new relationship when you are not in fellowship with an old one. So are you ready to reconcile? I thought you'd never ask. This is how we begin.

Directions: Please write a letter to someone you are out of fellowship with, asking them to forgive you of your trespass against them. Address it, stamp it and mail it immediately! For the perfect people of the group who have no trespasses against anyone and vice versa, please draft a letter anyway and file it, because at some point in your life you will be needing one!

Sample Letter:

Mr. Johnny Be Good
333 Happy Lane
Pleasantville, HI 77777

Dear Mr. Good:

I sincerely pray this letter finds you in good health and in good spirits. This letter serves to ask you to forgive me for not repaying you the loan in the amount of $1200 twenty years ago. Please accept the enclosed check of that amount with interest. It was my intention to repay you years ago.

Thank you again and please accept my humblest apology. I would love to hear from you and the family to catch up on everything. My telephone number is 787-303-0949. Thanks. May the Lord continue to bless your every endeavor.

In Christ,
Grace Mercy

Thank you for honoring the Lord by sending that letter to an individual you have something against. Now sit back and wait how the Lord is going to respond to your next need. Now that you have forgiven that individual or asked for forgiveness, you have freed yourself up to be blessed by God more abundantly than you could ever expect. There is something freeing about not owing any man anything but love. Whenever we harbor resentment over a sin committed against us, we are usually the only one affected by it. The offending individual probably has no concept of our feelings and if they did, they would more than likely not care. So release them.

I remember clearly having some negative feelings toward a sister in Christ who was, unbeknownst to her, my mentor. I watched this woman's life very closely. In fact, I emulated her in actions, words and deeds. I spoke very highly of her to everyone we encountered. I really respected her. So when I was experiencing a very traumatic time in my life I naturally confided in her and expected her to take my side in the situation. How devastated I was when she rebuked me and literally sided with my opponent. After taking me nearly a year to recover, I realized that I had set her up as the Lord of my life when in fact Jesus needed to be the one I confided in. He would never leave me nor forsake me. I should have measured the trials I was experiencing by the standards in God's Word, not by what human beings thought. This was an emotionally expensive lesson nevertheless, a very enlightening one. Now when I am in conflict with a life decision, I take it right to the throne of God and leave it there. He has never failed me yet!

Chapter Ten

Fruit of the Spirit

According to Galatians 5:22-26, "But the fruit of the Spirit is love, joy, peace, patience, kindness, goodness, faithfulness, gentleness and self-control. Against such things there is no law. Those who belong to Christ Jesus have crucified the sinful nature with its passions and desires. Since we live by the Spirit, let us keep in step with the Spirit. Let us not become conceited, provoking and envying each other."

These qualities are essential in our efforts to reconcile. Let's examine each one of these. Love is defined by Webster's New World Dictionary as "a deep affection for or attachment or devotion to someone, or the expression of this." While that is an appropriate definition for love, love for our fellow man is paramount to being a Christian. There is no surprise that this is the second greatest commandment spoken from the heart of Jesus. He was so passionate about this commandment that the greatest command was to love Him.

For this discussion we are going to need a more comprehensible interpretation. In the Greek text the highest form of love is called agape. It's God's unconditional love for fallen man. When we set out to love our fellow man who may be different than ourselves, we must recognize we cannot love him in our own strength. It takes a constant filling from God's Holy Spirit to enable us to love. For those of us with children, although they don't always act in accordance with our standards, we love them regardless of their behavior, it should be the same way with people of a different ethnicity. Just because they don't share your views of the world or have the same values you espouse doesn't mean you should love them any less.

How in the world do we, week after week, stand in churches all over America worshipping the Lord, lifting hands, singing praises and weeping uncontrollably and adoring a God in heaven we have never laid eyes on, and yet we sit next to a person of a different race and we are afraid to shake their hand? What's wrong with this picture?

When we get to heaven there won't be any "whites only" and "coloreds only" sections. We will all be mixed together. How disheartening it was for me the first time I moved to a suburb outside of Chicago when I was about fifteen. My first experience attending a church was horrifying. My mom and I visited a community church that was predominately Caucasian. As we approached the fourth pew in the front, a little gray-haired Caucasian woman who was adamant about the seat next to her insisted that someone else would be joining her momentarily. About an hour passed but her proposed friend never arrived. My mother and I to this very day have never walked back into that church. The woman's motives may have been purer than the driven snow. Even so, how could she have handled the situation differently?

When we love our brothers and sisters in Christ we choose to esteem them higher than ourselves. This love acted out places their best interest before ours. This type of love would lay down his life for a friend. Because Christ died on the cross for all of our sins, we also need to die to ourselves in attempting to reconcile cross-culturally. When a Christ follower is truly operating in this love, strife, misunderstandings and harsh words roll right off of your back.

When we demonstrate this agape love we will become ambassadors for reconciliation. It will flow through us naturally. We will serve each other with diligence and passion. When we rely on this form of love our reconciliation journey will be effortless. When we walk in this true anointing from the Lord, people will know and their enthusiasm for reconciliation will surface.

Love was such an important quality in the Bible that an entire chapter was devoted to the subject. In 1 Corinthians 13 we see that, "Love is patient, love is kind," and it suffers long. It endures through the most difficult times. True love never ends. It doesn't allow resentment over trivial matters to build up. When something is bothering you about a brother or sister in the Lord from a different culture, speak up compassionately. Resolve it by communicating and letting your request be made known. Don't allow the sun to go down on your wrath. When this quality is operating, each person talks it out and finds a solution each one can agree upon.

Love does not envy. Since we are all created in the image of God we should consider each other as unique and operating with different gifts. Love is not jealous of a special talent the other may possess. Love encourages and supports the other individual in their quest to live up to their fullest potential in Jesus Christ. It keeps all negative judgments to ourselves.

Love is not proud. Thinking you are better than someone else is a sin. Our only boast should be in the Lord. Let the Lord exalt you, because when He does, it lasts longer than man's adulation.

Love does not behave rudely. Just because you may have had a negative encounter with someone of a different race doesn't mean you need to retaliate against every member of that person's race. Love fails to ascribe the negative characteristics of one individual of a particular race to the entire culture. I am reminded of a woman in a former church who had been sexually violated by an African-American man. Right after her experience she would cringe anytime she had to interact with a black man, I think because it reminded her of the assailant. Her pastor actually assisted her with paying for therapy to help her overcome it. He was wise enough to know that this event, as horrific as it was, had the potential to further destroy and alienate African Americans in the congregation.

If love is of central concern, when we don't get our way we shouldn't have an attitude the rest of the day. The silent treatment should never be used as a weapon. If you are angry at an issue relating to racial reconciliation, perhaps you should retreat and regroup. We are never to respond in a critical, mean and evil-spirited way. We are to treat each other with respect, exactly like we would want to be treated.

Love is not easily angered. It doesn't fly off the handle with one hint of provocation but it covers a multitude of sins. When you love someone cross-culturally you will tolerate a lot of their faults and imperfections, especially since you have a few of your own shortcomings.

Love doesn't think evil of another or plan ill against them. It supports and encourages that person in the pursuit of all their goals. Love does not rejoice in iniquity, but rejoices in the truth. It rejoices in good, and grieves when another person is hurt or feeling defeated. It never envies others' praises, attention or honor. It won't put that other person down to build themselves up. It rejoices in that other person's achievements. Love trusts, hopes and preservers. It protects the other individual from the attacks of others. It doesn't entertain negative words about them. It doesn't gossip about their imperfections. Love is concerned about their character. It allows that individual to be who they were created by God to be. It seeks to do them good all the days of their life. It doesn't try to manipulate or control the other. Nor does it change them in any way. Love waits patiently for that person to grow. It remains constant no matter what the trial may be. It's a commitment that requires active participation.

Love never fails. Agape love is supported by a Savior who can do anything. We have to rely on this notion and move outside our comfort zone. When all the churches across the world realize that agape love is the missing ingredient in racial reconciliation, there will be a revival first in the church and secondly throughout the land. Watch the world join us when they see Christians coming together in harmony and living peaceably side by side. They will see that maybe this Christianity has some validity to it. They will run to God seeking repentance because they will know that only a God like ours could ever accomplish such a great task. In the process they may come to reconcile with Jesus Christ which, after all, is the greater good.

The second fruit of the Spirit is joy. According to Nehemiah 8:10, "'Go and enjoy choice food and sweet drinks, and send some to those who have nothing prepared. This day is sacred to our Lord. Do not grieve, for the joy of the Lord is your strength.'" A daily dosage of joy will be needed to combat defeat when trying to reconcile cross-culturally. You will need a joyous disposition to effectively deal with the challenges associated with human beings regardless of what culture they belong to. There will be times when you will need to choose joy when confronted or misunderstood.

Whenever you discern potential for hostilities, you need to whisper a prayer of protection to the Lord. There are activities I weekly participate in that I know have the possibility of being volatile if I allow the devil a foothold. As a result, just before I enter a grocery store, I serve the devil and all his demons notice that "no weapon forged against me shall prosper." I am more than a conqueror. I am blessed in the city. I am blessed in the field. I am the head and not the tail above and not below." Next time you are tempted to fly off the handle try confessing who you are to the devil.

Joy also encompasses having a sense of humor. Lighten up! Have yourself some fun. Always try to see the bright side of things. Remember the Scripture reference in Psalm 30:5, "Weeping may remain for a night, but rejoicing comes in the morning." No matter what curve balls life throws at you, there is absolutely no circumstance that we face that could harm us without first going through our Lord. He buffets every trial and tribulation we face. He is always there. According to Jeremiah 29:11, He promises, "'For I know the plans I have for you,' declares the Lord, 'plans to prosper you and not to harm you, plans to give you hope and a future.'"

When racing towards reconciliation a sense of humor is necessary. There will be times when you will need to see the humor in your interactions. I vividly remember my college days when many of the students had never seen an African American before except on television. I had to laugh because they were treating me as if I was a rare artifact. While I must admit I enjoyed the attention, sometimes their ignorance concerning my culture was very annoying. I recall the first time we all went out to dinner. I ordered liver and rice for dinner, while many of them ordered hamburger and fries. Since they were pretty amazed about my selection of cuisine I thought I would intensify their bewilderment. The waiter received all of the orders and returned to ask me how I would like my liver fried. I smiled and added, "Oh, you fry it here. I was planning to eat it raw." My classmates didn't know whether to laugh or display disgust. It wasn't until I broke out into a wide grin that they realized I was joking. By having a sense of humor they welcomed me as any other member of their family. So laugh!

I also remember another encounter with a two-year-old who had apparently never seen an African American. There she was, this cute blue-eyed toddler with curly blonde hair, walking up to me at the community swimming pool. All of a sudden she feverishly tried to wipe my arm. The mother ran over to rescue her as she began to cry hysterically. When the mom asked what the matter was, she said, "I am trying to wash the dirt off of the lady's arm but it won't come off." The mother turned at least three shades redder and reprimanded her child. I laughed. The people around me didn't know how to respond. The mother shamefully admitted that I was the first African American her daughter had ever seen in real life. To which I responded, "I am not offended at her words. What offends me is the fact you have never sought out friendships with African Americans so your daughter wouldn't have this experience. May I suggest you provide her with some exposure of different cultures while she is moldable?" The mother smiled, thanked me and jumped into the pool.

About ten minutes later she extended to us an invitation to play with her children the following week at their home. To this very day the mom remains one of my very good friends. You see, if I hadn't laughed but had become offended about this child's curiosity, I would have deprived this child, her family and my family of an opportunity to reconcile cross-culturally. See how important the oil of joy is in racial reconciliation?

The third fruit of the Spirit is peace. According to Colossians 3:15 we are to "let the peace of Christ rule in your hearts, since as members of one body you were called to peace. And be thankful." The peace of Christ involves a calm, quiet state of being, serenity and the ability to live in harmony with oneself and others around you. If you are at peace you can walk on turbulent water like Jesus did and the winds and the waves will obey you. According to Isaiah 43:2, "When you pass through the waters, I will be with you; and when you pass through the rivers, they will not sweep over you. When you walk through the fire, you will not be burned; the flames will not set you ablaze." That's an individual walking in peace. A total assurance that God has your best interest at heart at all times.

When you are racing towards reconciliation you are cool, calm and collected. There will be occasions when someone may force you to display your emotions. Yet because of the grace extended to you from God, you will choose to respond in a clam, gentle manner. For example, the devil knows our weaknesses. He studies and observes what we value the most and attacks us there. He knows I can be offended by people all day long and it will roll right off of my back. However, he knows that when it comes to my children, I don't play! So being the slimy, cunning, manipulating and crafty snake he is, he plots ways to offend me using my children as ransom. And to make matters worse, he uses other Christians for his schemes.

It was a cold winter day in December and I was visiting a new church. I did my homework and called them to inform them that I would be bringing my special needs daughter in this particular Sunday. They said it would be okay and they would arrange more staff so they could have someone specifically to aid her. I proceeded to the church nursery, racing my daughter in her wheelchair. One of the teachers stopped me at the door and told me, "We don't take handicapped children." Being totally caught off guard, I insisted she repeat what she said, just in case I had misunderstood her. And again she repeated the phrase as clearly as she had the first time. It was such a devastating blow to my heart that I had to remind myself to breathe. After informing her that Jesus would never deny a child He created entrance into a Sunday school class I walked away.

By the time church was over I was a complete nervous wreck. Since I had held my emotions in for two hours I felt I had earned the right to explode. When I walked past the classroom, the Lord instructed me to teach her and not to alienate her. I asked her if this was church policy and did the leadership support this. She became obstinate about my inquiry and, when I determined she was not cooperative, I asked to see the leader. By the time he appeared a steady flow of tears was falling down my face like the falls at Niagara. The leader displayed less compassion than she did. By the time the entire event was over, I discovered I was the villain.

That was the most difficult experience I've ever encountered concerning discrimination, and the saddest part of it was the fact it was an African-American fellow believer who was perpetrating the evil-spirited deed.

Though I defined peace as a calm, quiet state of being and the ability to live in harmony with others, I am not sure I was operating in that definition at the time. But I was able to keep my emotions in check. However, drastic circumstances call for drastic measures. In this instance it was my responsibility to address the discrimination, especially since these were fellow Christians. Wasn't it Jesus who told us in His Word on many occasions that, according to Matthew 18:6, "'But if anyone causes one of these little ones who believe in me to sin, it would be better for him to have a large millstone hung around his neck and to be drowned in the depths of the sea.'"

In reconciling cross-culturally we need to keep the peace. The only time we need to confront someone is when the greater good of the individual would be to speak up. When in doubt, consult the Word of God.

The fourth fruit of the Spirit is patience. I am always reminded of the sense of urgency that I have for patience. I want patience and I need it most immediately! Webster's New World Dictionary defines patience as "enduring pain, trouble, etc. with composure and without complaint, calmly tolerating insult, delay, and confusion." This is a very important part of our daily routine. I cannot tell you the numerous occasions I've had to practice this quality. Anybody with children knows you have to exercise patience at all times when dealing with them. In reconciling cross-culturally patience is more than a virtue. It's a requirement. We have to endure whatever challenges we face as calmly as possible. African Americans should have this down to a science seeing how we've had to practice it all of our lives. We've had to hold our peace even when our flesh wanted to throw a tantrum. Some of us literally had to ask God to restrain us when we were confronted with racism.

Patience requires that you count to ten before responding to someone. I vividly recall a trip to Florida where I went to Spring Training to watch the Atlanta Braves. I arrived at my seat near the dugout where a group of Caucasian men and women were thoroughly annoyed that I had better seats than they did. And to top it off I had to inconvenience them by making them stand up in order for me to get to my seat. By the time I arrived at the end of the row, one of the guys yelled down to his wife that I was about to sit next to her and instructed her to pick up her purse that was on the ground (as if I wanted it). I must tell you exercising patience in that circumstance was quite challenging. I really had to restrain myself. I had to encourage myself in the Lord and remind myself Whose daughter I was.

Patience not only involves self-restraint but is also an attribute needed to deal with individuals cross-culturally. There will be times when you are in relationship with someone and you will need to exercise patience because their way of doing things are totally different than yours. For example, what if you are organizing an event that begins at 9:00 a.m. and your expectation for everyone participating would be that they arrive at 8:45 to help set up. Well what if the African Americans you are trying to reconcile with think they are required to arrive by 9:00 a.m. or shortly thereafter? Clearly you have two individuals with two different expectations. (Some African Americans are generally late to everything. They tell me it's a cultural thing and I wouldn't understand. So if you want us to be there at 9:00 say 8:45). How are you going to exercise patience in this instance?

Patience requires a deliberate crucifying of the flesh. When we have this quality, we communicate to the individual that whatever comes my way regarding your behavior I will choose to actively pursue a calm, tolerant delay of immediate self-gratification. It lovingly communicates to them that their needs are your primary concern and that you are willing to place your own desires on hold to honor theirs.

The fifth fruit of the Spirit is kindness. This quality is described as the ability to be sympathetic, friendly and gentle. When this characteristic is played out in the life of an individual, they will seek not to change the other person. It bears with that person, supporting and believing in their dreams. Kindness is exercising good manners by being considerate of the other's needs. For example, if you are trying to relate cross-culturally and you are making a decision to socialize, you may not be fond of their entertainment selection. In fact, you may be radically opposed. Unless it is immoral, unethical or clearly against God's Word, you should enthusiastically participate.

I remember receiving an invitation to a hockey game from one of my Caucasian friends. Hockey was definitely not my cup of cappuccino, but because I was trying to place their needs higher than mine I consented to the event. Initially I was very uncomfortable with the whole premise of grown men hitting each other with sticks and knocking each other's lights out. But after a few minutes into the game I genuinely began to enjoy it. My sacrificial act of considering the needs of my Caucasian friend opened his heart for reconciliation. He was impressed that I would consider his needs before my own.

Kindness also involves responding with gentleness to someone who offends you. I am truly amazed at all the false assumptions Caucasians still make about us. I count it a joy and a great privilege to impart wisdom to them. Recently a man shared with me that the African-American children his son attends school with are immoral. He had the audacity to ask me if it was a cultural thing. I had to ask the Lord for that kindness fruit immediately. And as soon as it kicked in I responded, "Certainly you don't think all African-American children are immoral. Have you known any Caucasians, Hispanic or Asian people who lack positive moral development? I am just willing to hypothesize that there is a segment of people represented in every culture who need assistance with character development. So perhaps we are referring to a sin problem and not a skin one."

Kindness allows me to dispel any stereotypes against us with a calm and gentle spirit, always remembering Who I serve.

The sixth fruit of the Spirit is goodness. Please allow me to place gentleness in the same category as goodness. Gentleness and goodness are synonymous. You cannot have one without the other. Goodness is a gentle disposition towards others. When you are operating in gentleness Christ should be evident in your life. You should have the ability to be polite, kind, patient and generous.

In reconciling cross-culturally we are required to be polite. To insist on doing things your way instead of extending your fellow brother or sister an opportunity to assist you is discourteous. You need to consult them and devise a plan that meets both parties' needs. When you are gentle you are quiet and meek. You are compassionate when dealing with conflict. You are soft spoken and very flexible. When you are gentle you are always behaving in a way that glorifies the Lord. You use your manners saying please, thank you, no sir, and yes ma'am as the situation dictates. You are always gracious, humble and wise when you use this quality.

Goodness is the activity that results from being kind. It's an outward experience of your inner self. When operating in goodness you are a blessing to others. You are friendly and smile. You have a tender heart towards others and see them as mattering to God. When you are walking in goodness you immediately repent when you sin. You are open to the Lord molding your character. If someone is abrasive concerning you, this quality will soften your disposition towards them. Goodness allows you to interact with others who will literally take notice of who you are. Your witness to the world will demand an explanation when you are committed to full devotion and this quality manifests itself in your life. This quality will radiate from you so greatly that the unsaved world will desperately want what you have. Goodness is also evident in your character. As a good person you are righteous, holy and pure. You won't visit places of ill repute, you won't gossip or entertain it. You are pure in all actions, words and deeds. When we exercise goodness in our lives we will reap what we sow. Our Lord will extend to us the same goodness we extend to others.

Faithfulness is the seventh fruit of the Spirit. It is described as being loyal, responsible and keeping the faith. When a person is faithful they are determined to adhere to any cause they champion. Faithfulness in racial reconciliation is paramount. It is a necessity because of the difficult challenges associated with it. There is a tremendous need for both individuals to have loyalty for this cause. Faithfulness demands that if you are mentoring African-American children on a Saturday morning at 9:00 a.m. that you are there consistently week after week, month after month, year after year. Imagine the disappointment that will arise when you arrive only at your convenience.

Faithfulness will cause you to apologize to an African American if they are offended by you or someone else. Faithfulness requires that we make restitution on some else's behalf. It also encourages responsibility. You will be committed to carrying out acts of reconciliation with excellence, diligence and integrity. You will be fully devoted to your goals, seeking to please the Lord in all areas of your life. When this quality is in full operation the individual has a sense of peace, gratitude and fulfillment that the Lord is completing a good work in their lives.

The final fruit of the Spirit quality is self-control. This is one of the most difficult traits for me to master when relating cross-culturally. I personally feel this is one of the most important fruits in an individual's life. The ability to exercise self-restraint is a key ingredient in racing towards reconciliation. Without the ability to control your own emotions when confronted with discrimination, racism, sexism, nationalism, classism or any other isms that separate us, you will cripple any attempts at healing. By nature we are fleshly creatures preoccupied with self-gratification in our physical appetites. And it is a daily press to bring our flesh under subjection.

If our beloved King David in 2 Samuel 11:2-16 exercised self-control he would have not endured the painful consequences of his sin. In verse 2 we see, “One evening David got up from his bed and walked around on the roof of the palace. From the roof he saw a woman bathing. The woman was very beautiful, and David sent someone to find out about her. The man said, ‘Isn’t this Bathsheba, the daughter of Eliam and the wife of Uriah the Hittite?’ Then David sent messengers to get her. She came to him, and he slept with her. (She had purified herself from her uncleanness.) Then she went back home. The woman conceived and sent word to David, saying, ‘I am pregnant.’ So David sent this word to Joab: ‘Send me Uriah the Hittite.’ And Joab sent him to David. When Uriah came to him, David asked him how Joab was, how the soldiers were and how the war was going. Then David said to Uriah, ‘Go down to your house and wash your feet.’ So Uriah left the palace, and a gift from the king was sent after him. But Uriah slept at the entrance to the palace with all his master’s servants and did not go down to his house. When David was told, ‘Uriah did not go home,’ he asked him, ‘Haven’t you just come from a distance? Why didn’t you go home?’ Uriah said to David, ‘The ark and Israel and Judah are staying in tents, and my master Joab and my lord’s men are camped in the open fields. How could I go to my house to eat and drink and lie with my wife? As surely as you live, I will not do such a thing!’”

The rest of the story unfolds with David sending Uriah to the front line of combat where he was killed. Not only did David commit adultery, but he was also responsible for murdering Uriah to cover up an unplanned pregnancy. Just think if David had turned away the minute he saw Bathsheba bathing on the roof, we would not be reading about his life in the book of Samuel. The moment he saw her he should have resisted the devil, and the devil would have fled from him. By not exercising self-control he succumbed to the temptation. He hadn’t read James 1:13-15 to know “when tempted, no one should say ‘God is tempting me.’ For God cannot be tempted by evil, nor does he tempt anyone; but each one is tempted when, by his own evil desire, he is dragged away and enticed. Then, after desire has conceived, it gives birth to sin; and sin, when it is full-grown, gives birth to death.”

When David saw girlfriend on the roof he should have immediately changed the channel. By continuing to observe her, his flesh overpowered him. Even Jesus was tempted while in the desert. The difference was He always applied the Word of God to His situation which delivered Him from the evil. When David committed adultery the sin stripped him from his anointing. The call God had on his life was tainted by his sin. Of course when he repented, he was fully restored in right standing and became known as a man after God’s own heart. Nevertheless, he still had to pay the consequences for his actions. David lost his son and experienced devastation in his leadership. Even though God loved him, He still had to chasten him.

In cross-cultural reconciliation we cannot afford to allow the devil to steal all God has for us. If you are seeking a cross-cultural fellowship with a member of the opposite sex, please be careful. If you are married, this needs to be a joint effort with your spouse. If the individual is a single female, let your wife initiate the relationship. If the individual is male and single, the husband should initiate the interaction. Satan stays up all night devising schemes to make us fall. He’s especially crafty in the area of racial reconciliation because he knows the potential power we have in Jesus if we are all on one accord.

When interacting cross-culturally with the opposite sex, the rule of thumb I always adhere to is to treat the individual as a fellow brother in the Lord and respect him as such. If you are ever attracted to someone who is not your spouse, immediately confess your sin to God and ask Him to deliver you from the lust of the flesh. And stop the pursuit. Remind Satan that you are not ignorant of his devices. Tell him to go back to where he came from. If the stronghold is more powerful than you are, fast and pray, because our spirits are willing but our flesh is weak. That is the reason Jesus tells us in Matthew 5:28, "'But I tell you that anyone who looks at a woman lustfully has already committed adultery with her in his heart.'" He spoke that because he knew as soon as we entertained the thought we would progress into the activity based on the power of suggestion. The devil presents us with a glimpse of a thought that we play over and over in our minds like a broken record until we actually feel compelled to bring it to fruition.

The trick of Satan is to deceive us. In that deception he may present an ounce of truth to convince us that the thought is from God. For example, when he deceived Eve in the Garden of Eden he said, "Did God really say, 'You may not eat from any tree in the garden?'" He twisted the truth by asking her to clarify what God said. And although Eve was able to repeat what God said, the devil approached her from a different perspective by concocting a reason God didn't want her to partake of the fruit in the forbidden garden—that she would be as wise as God. Just in one confrontation Satan tempted Eve on three different levels. The first was appetite—she saw the fruit of the tree was good for food. The second was sight—it was pleasing to the eye. The third was pride—it was for gaining wisdom. Eve should have restrained herself to the boundaries the Lord had already put in place. In fact, when she saw the Enemy she shouldn't have given him the time of day. She should have enslaved her body by telling it what to do, not allowing her thoughts to control her. She could have strengthened her inner man by quoting to the devil what the Lord instructed her to do repetitively until it manifested itself in her mind. She should have determined to fulfill God's instructions.

Another area we must control is our emotions. As a woman I am very aware of my hormonal imbalances at certain times of the month. But instead of my hormones ruling me I place them in subjection to my mind. Whenever thoughts of depression or irritability arrive I talk to myself. I confess to my body that I am walking in complete health, peace, wholeness and joy until my body catches up with the words I am speaking.

Racial reconciliation is not for the faint of heart. Especially not for individuals who are very sensitive. You have to have very thick skin, because your risk of being misunderstood, rejected and even persecuted are very great. So if you are the type of person who cries the moment you are challenged, or you don't like people pointing out your faults, or you are easily offended, you need to champion another cause!

In racial reconciliation you will be dealing with many volatile issues. There are hurts and wounds that are very painful and deep in others' lives as well as your own. There may be early childhood experiences you may not want to revisit. It could be catastrophic when you are confronted by an individual with a totally different perspective than yours. There will be places where no man has gone before. Are you ready for that? Are your emotions in check? Are you in control or will you have to constantly restrain yourself when people speak the truth in love to you?

To my African-American brothers and sisters, I feel your pain. In fact, I share it. But we have to take the road less traveled concerning racial reconciliation. Whenever we are challenged in areas of discrimination we are required by the Lord to exercise self-restraint. We become worse than our transgressors if we give place to the devil. The next time you are challenged, remember Whose you are and the call God has on your life. Verbally confess all known sin when you fall short of the mark. And by all means, pray without ceasing.

Since you are feeling very fruitful, you are ripe for our next exercises.

Case Studies

Directions: Read each case study. Apply the fruit of the Spirit action to it and describe why you chose that response.

CASE STUDY #1—As a Caucasian employer you decide to hire an African-American homeless man for security detail at your factory. There have been several reports that he's been sleeping on the job. When you confront him, he denies the accusations and threatens you with a racial discrimination suit if you terminate him.

What fruit of the Spirit quality will you use?
I would use self-control, because I am very angry that a man more qualified for this position applied and I accepted this man because I wanted to give him a chance. I cannot believe he has the audacity to accuse me of racism when in fact he's just not doing his job properly. I need self-control and I need it right this minute! In fact he's ruined it for other homeless people. I will never hire another one!

How does the employer really feel?
He is justifiably angry. He gave a man a chance and instead of the man being grateful for the opportunity, he insulted his employer by falsely accusing him.

Is he justified in his emotions?
Of course he is. Wouldn't you be?

What would you do given the same circumstances?
I would terminate him immediately and not allow another one of those people to step foot into my factory again.

What does God's Word say about this incident?
The Word of God says we need to forgive those who trespass against us. But I am only human.
(This is an example of how *not* to reconcile cross-culturally. Please rewrite this entire scenario in the available spaces.)

CASE STUDY #2—You're an African-American couple who recently married. You and your spouse decide to rent a portion of your home to an unwed, pregnant Caucasian mother. After her second week she decides she doesn't have to follow the rules anymore, even though she signed a lease agreement. She plays loud music, entertains different men every night and her living quarters are filthy. You both decide to confront her. She storms away from the meeting and threatens she will seek revenge if you evict her. The following day you arrive home from work and your entire house is trashed.

What fruit of the Spirit quality would you use at that moment?

What emotions are you experiencing?

Are you justified in your emotions?

What does God's Word say about how to deal with the incident?

CASE STUDY #3—You're an interracial couple wanting to be married at the church you've attended for over twenty years. When you seek out premarital counseling, the pastor informs you that interracial marriages are not supported biblically. He also tells you that he cannot marry you with a clear conscience. He opens his Bible and cites three different references he thinks support his claim.

What fruit of the Spirit quality would you use?

What does the Bible have to say regarding interracial marriages?

Would you confront this pastor?

Would you seek premarital counseling elsewhere?

Would you remain at that particular church?

CASE STUDY #4—You're a Caucasian couple who desperately wants to adopt African-American children. You decide to provide foster care for a sibling group of three. After falling in love with the children, the social worker informs you that the biological parents, who are both African American, decided that the children should be adopted by an African-American family. Even though you informed the agency you would adopt them all, the social worker thinks it is more beneficial for another family to adopt them.

Which fruit of the Spirit quality do you need? More than one quality can be used.

Are there any legal recourses you could explore?

What are your other options?

Should you pursue justice in this case?

What does God's Word say about this situation?

CASE STUDY #5—You're a recent African-American male college graduate currently searching for employment. Aware of the challenges associated with locating employment, you exceed the expectations by dressing extremely well. You are also prepared by rehearsing with another human resource professional on how to interview. You ace the exams and your interview was quite successful. As you leave, you overhear two Caucasian male candidates say, "We don't have a chance. They will probably hire the black guy. You know they get all the favor because of affirmative action. I wish I was black."

What fruit of the Spirit quality would you use?

Would you ignore or react to their words?

As an African American, how would you feel about being offered the position because of your race?

If you ever thought you were being hired for a position because of your race, would you accept it? Why or why not?

CASE STUDY #6 — You're an African-American female disc jockey at the number one station in a metropolitan city. During a Christmas party, the Caucasian male sidekick on your program is slightly inebriated and blurts out his salary, which is twice as much as what you earn.

What fruit of the Spirit quality would you use?

Should you confront management regarding the discrepancy?

Are there any legal ramifications you can explore?

Does this appear to be a gender or racial issue?

CASE STUDY #7 — You're an African-American family who purchased a home in an affluent suburb. While you're shopping for new furniture you arrive home and someone has spray-painted derogatory racial epithets on your garage.

What fruit of the Spirit quality would you use?

Would you contact law enforcement authorities?

Would you pursue criminal charges?

Would you report this discrimination to the Civil Rights Commission?

Would you immediately move out of the neighborhood?

CASE STUDY #8 — You're a young single Caucasian woman who is expecting an interracial baby. Your parents have abandoned you and insist on the termination of your pregnancy.

What fruit of the Spirit qualities will you need to deal with your parents?

What are your options for the pregnancy?

What should you do concerning your pregnancy?

Find four Scripture verses that deal with choosing life for an unplanned pregnancy and write them down.

1.
2.
3.
4.

Please give a donation or volunteer your time at a pro-life Crisis Pregnancy Center.

CASE STUDY #9—You're a Caucasian man who enjoys worshipping in an African-American church. There's an African-American woman who appears to be interested in you. After conversing with her for more than two hours you conclude she is unequally yoked with you. You are more spiritually mature than her. Clearly you know marriage would never be an option, yet you insist that reconciling cross-culturally is more important than her lack of spiritual maturity.

What fruit of the Spirit quality should you consider?

Is it ever okay to marry someone who is a Christian but not spiritually mature?

Should you continue being her friend?

Should you continue being involved with her?

Role Play Exercise

Directions: Now that you are a master at exercising these nine fruit of the Spirit qualities, let's see how well you do in another role-play activity. Respond to these real life situations as an African American.

DRAMA ONE: What Goes Up Must Get Off

You are an African-American male who gets on an elevator with an elderly Caucasian woman. The moment she sees you she clutches her purse and exits right before the door closes.

- **Discuss the implications of the woman's actions.**
- **How should the man respond to the woman's actions?**
- **Is there any way her actions could have been misinterpreted?**
- **What would be your response if this happened to you?**

DRAMA TWO: Check This Out

You are an African-American woman in the grocery store checkout line. Once you secure your groceries, the Caucasian cashier asks you if you are planning to pay in cash or food stamps.

- **What did the cashier assume about the woman?**
- **How did she arrive at this conclusion?**
- **Was that an appropriate response for the woman?**
- **Is confrontation appropriate in this situation?**

DRAMA THREE: Red Light, Green Light

You are an African-American, sixteen-year-old male who observes red, flashing lights in your rearview mirror. You pull over and the Caucasian policeman is quite abrasive towards you even though you obeyed all the traffic rules.

- **Was the policeman justified in pulling the teen over?**
- **How should the teenager have responded to the policeman's attitude?**
- **Should the teenager report the police officer?**
- **If that was your son and he arrived home upset, how would you console him?**

DRAMA FOUR: No Place Like Home

You are a single African-American mother with your three well-behaved children trying to rent a house from a Caucasian male. Once you arrived he suddenly remembers that he is considering someone else for the home.

- **Were the children a hindrance to the mother's ability to rent the home?**
- **Were there any other variables that would prevent the owner from renting the property to her?**
- **Does she have any legal recourse?**
- **What would you do in this situation?**

DRAMA FIVE: Stand in Front of Me

You are an African-American man standing in line at the public library, and the Caucasian librarian, aware of your turn, decides to ask the Caucasian woman behind you if she needs assistance.

- **What were the implications of the librarian's actions?**
- **What should've been the response of the patron's in the line observing? How about the patron who didn't wait her turn?**
- **Should the African-American man ignore the action?**
- **Should he speak up?**

DRAMA SIX: Are You Watching Me Now?

You are an African-American woman at a department store, and as soon as you walk through the doors you are accosted by several Caucasian sales people who insist on helping you. As you browse you observe that you are getting much more attention than desirable. As you begin to make clothing selections, you notice a security officer is following you around the store, and you make a comment about how you are annoyed at their actions.

- **Did the African-American woman respond correctly to the security officer?**
- **Was the security officer justified in his actions?**
- **If you were employed at this department store, would you have responded in the same manner? What if your manager insisted that you do?**
- **Why were the other Caucasian customers treated differently than the African-American woman?**

Chapter Eleven

Where Do We Grow from Here?

I am always amazed when people talk about a subject that is as volatile as race, how they can identify the problem yet not give any solutions on how to effectively remedy it. With a subject as massive as the one we just tackled, I am not anticipating I can do significant justice to it myself. But I will surely try. Let's explore a few of these proactive steps we can take in our quest to race towards reconciliation. They are intentionally unnumbered because the sequencing doesn't matter. What matters is that you try them. Many of these will be repeated from other parts of the book since repetition aids learning.

Acknowledge racism exists by being sensitive to our plight. Just because you've never personally experienced a negative encounter regarding race relations doesn't necessarily mean it hasn't occurred. Remember, if you had a heart ailment, there is no doctor who would release you without a battery of tests, even if you have *one* symptom, unless you signed a consent form.

There is a problem, not a skin problem but a sin problem, and we have evidence in the social, political, educational, and economical arenas that indicate some people are experiencing pain. Jesus won't deny us treatment when He has a signed covenant in His blood that authorizes every Christ follower the capacity to assist in his own healing. The wavier is the Bible which clearly communicates to us how to live in harmony with all men.

We really can do this! We can learn to be empathetic towards someone even when we cannot identify with them. I've seen this in operation countless times. Our most recent example was when September 11, 2001 occurred. There was a tremendous outpouring of love and compassion. I heard stories of Christians assisting Muslims with grocery store chores because many of the women were afraid to leave their homes because of feared retaliation. We had such an overabundance of blood donated that the Red Cross had to turn people away. We were able to raise millions of dollars. So please don't tell me when there is a tragedy that we cannot bond for the common good of all. So why don't we liken racial disunity to the event of September 11 and label it as a national tragedy and work together to annihilate it?

Repent from your negative attitudes. Even though you don't feel motivated to say you're sorry for the sins of your forefathers, surely you can apologize for the current state of racial tensions in the twenty-first century. You could at least admit that there is a strong possibility that we are not making this stuff up. If we are, there are thousands of other people with the same story. The lack of compassion stems from pride and arrogance. If you clothe yourself with humility and come before the Savior's throne and repent, what freedom you will experience! Imagine the grace, mercy and favor you will receive when you approach reconciliation from a servant's perspective. Just as Jesus washed the feet of His disciples, we ought to wash each other's feet.

Reconcile to Jesus first. If you are serious about reconciling cross-culturally and you haven't already reconciled to Jesus Christ, that should be the first order of business. According to John 3:16-17, "'For God so loved the world that he gave his one and only Son, that whoever believes in him shall not perish but have eternal life. For God did not send his Son into the world to condemn the world, but to save the world through Him.'" This Scripture clearly reveals the intent God had for His Son, Jesus, on our behalf. It is difficult enough as mature followers of Christ to reconcile cross-culturally. Imagine how much more difficult this task is when we don't have the power of the Holy Spirit working in us. If there is anyone who has not made that step of faith and would like to receive Jesus Christ as their personal Savior according to Romans 10:9 which states, "That if you confess with your mouth, 'Jesus is Lord,' and believe in your heart that God raised him from the dead, you will be saved," do so.

Are you ready to take this step of faith? If you verbally confess you believe that Jesus is Lord, and you know He died on the cross for your sins, ask Him to come into your heart and become the head of your life. Once you have done this, attend a local Bible-teaching church in your community and they will assist you with the rest of your spiritual growth.

Please feel free to contact the author at agapeproductions@sbcglobal.net if you have any additional questions about your new spiritual journey.

Pray without ceasing. Prayer is something you cannot do without. In order for your journey to be successful, you will need a very active prayer life. You will need continuous guidance from the Lord. More importantly you will need to be a good listener as the Lord speaks to you regarding His will for your life. If you have the gift of intercessory prayer and know how to combat against spiritual warfare, please stand on the front line and go to battle on our behalf and uphold those of us who are actively engaged in this journey. We have a prayer request form on our Web site. Please post your prayer request at agapeproductionsinc.com.

Initiate racial reconciliation by seeking out meaningful relationships cross-culturally. We fear what we don't understand, so make a concerted effort to establish meaningful lifetime friendships with members of the African-American community. Be intentional, take risks. Be the first one to initiate fellowship. No one likes rejection but sometimes it is a necessary means to an end. If you are an introvert, ask your small group members to band together to approach someone you would enjoy doing life with. Go for it!

Become actively involved in the African-American community. Commit yourself and your family to sacrificial acts of service. How about spending an entire day serving in the African-American community at least once a month? I know we are all busy. We make time for other activities. How about the next time you run Susie to her ballet class you take an African-American girl with you? How about taking an African-American teenage boy to a baseball or basketball game the next time you and your son hang out? You see, it takes minimal effort especially since you are already participating in these events.

Begin a mentoring program. How about organizing a tutorial program for African-American children to receive educational assistance from a positive role model? There could also be opportunities for business men in the community to adopt an African-American student to serve as an apprentice with the goal of teaching them how to start and operate their own successful business or corporation.

Start a parenting program. How about teaching a weekly class on issues relating to parenting for African-American and Caucasian young mothers? You can also organize a free Saturday morning babysitting service to give them some quiet time for themselves. How many of us know that parenting is very stressful? What a blessing we can be to these women who may be overwhelmed and possibly overburdened by their responsibilities.

Attend an African-American worship service. Will you be in for a treat if you take the time to visit an African-American church service! I guarantee you there is nothing else like this experience. You will be amazed by how different our services are from those of mainstream America. But don't let me influence you. Judge for yourself.

Join an African-American church. Why not, after attending an African-American worship service for a significant amount of time and evaluation, if you are called by God, join it?

Join an African-American book club. If you are an avid reader and African-American history is one of your passions, why not start a monthly book club where you and a few of your very good friends can dissect books relating specifically to and about black culture and authored by African Americans?

Join an African-American social or recreational club. Have you ever considered becoming a member of a social or recreational club that is predominately comprised of African-American individuals? There are a host of clubs you are welcome to join. The interests are as varied as sky diving and needlepoint.

Start a racially diverse play group for your children. Have you ever considered starting a play group with children from other communities beside your own?

Join a small group that discusses racial reconciliation. Or, if none exist near you, start your own. In churches across America this is an untapped resource. *Our greatest fears concerning racial reconciliation are conceived out of ignorance. But once we give birth to the truth, the Lord will hold us accountable.* If our churches are lacking in this area, there are ways you can approach the leadership in a respectable way to assist them in recognizing this problem. Many churches just don't have a clue that they may need to be more proactive. Their philosophy is, "If the Lord wants this church integrated He will add to the church daily as He sees fit." The only problem with this is the failure to realize that there is an intentional element involved. Another reason may be that the leadership may think that they cannot possibly be all things to all people. While that may be true, it doesn't hold much weight in this context. The intent of the former statement is when you try to appease everyone, there will be a small segment of society who will not appreciate your diligence. This concept is quite different because there is no attempt to appeal to a wider segment of society. For example, if your church is having a special program for married couples on Valentine's Day and they do nothing special for singles on the same day, there is a problem with that. The same concept applies to us. Week after week African Americans sit in white churches strongly encouraged to listen to their worship music and their preaching style with no attempt to bring in a diverse music style or an African-American pastor to speak. Let's be more sensitive.

Advocate for human rights. How about lobbying in Congress on behalf of political groups and organizations which seek to promote economical empowerment and equality? Or start your own organization.

Visit African-American cultural centers. During Black History Month there are a wealth of cultural events and activities throughout major cities. An invaluable resource is your local newspaper, libraries and the Internet. You can also visit many of the museums, civic centers, fine arts theaters and local colleges any time of the year.

Attend lectures on African-American history. Again during Black History Month there should be a wealth of information regarding lectures in your local community. Colleges and universities are usually places where these lectures are held. Occasionally the local libraries will sponsor one. Churches are increasingly becoming aware of the need and are beginning to open their doors for these series.

Hire African-American professionals to manage your corporation and serve as board members. The next time you have an opening in management or on the executive level of your corporation, hire an African-American individual to fill this position, even if there are no tax benefits. If you don't know any qualified individuals, contact me. I have an entire list of candidates I can recommend. The next time there is an opening on your board of directors, why not consider appointing an African American? I also have a national list of qualified individuals. Additionally, if there are African Americans who want to start their own company, why not consider making an investment in their vision? I also have a list of start-up companies needing investors.

Finance an African-American high school student's college education. Remember, the younger generation will be ruling our world very soon. Why not make an investment now that will pay huge dividends later on? Finance or assist an African-American student with their college expenses. Even something as minimal as buying their books for them would be a great blessing.

Take an African-American family on vacation with you. Many of you are blessed with summer homes and time shares. Why not invest some of your vacation time in getting better acquainted with an African-American family? Or perhaps you can allow them full disposal of your vacation home one week out of the year.

Write letters to missionaries serving in predominantly African-American countries or the inner city. What a great witnessing tool this is to your family when you all sit down and write a letter to our heroes in the mission field.

Provide a foster or adoptive home for African-American children. Every state has a program where there are several thousand children each year waiting to be adopted by a loving family. Why not open your heart and your home to these precious gifts from the Lord? There is even a tremendous need for single-parent homes. And senior citizens, you can serve as adopted grandparents to these orphans.

Organize a free concert featuring an African-American artist. Have a block party in your neighborhood and invite several hundred of your closest friends to hear a concert featuring a local African-American artist or possibly someone who is well known. You would be surprised by how many local celebrities would perform free as long as you pay their expenses. Besides, it never hurts to ask.

Organize a multicultural carnival-like fair where food and wares are featured from various cultures. With the support of your church, how about organizing a community-wide event that includes carnival rides, food and entertainment?

Organize a summer sports camp for African-American children. Most children enjoy sports activities. Why not host a summer sports camp featuring instruction in baseball, basketball, volleyball, football, soccer and golf? At the completion of each activity the children can enjoy a nutritious snack and a short devotional.

Organize a dance class for African-American children. Children enjoy movement. Why not secure the services of a professional dancer who could teach them how to dance creatively? Formal instructions could also be given at no charge.

Organize a speech or debate team for African-American youth. Many of these children may not be exposed to public speaking opportunities. What a tremendous benefit this program can be to assist them with developing their intellect and their speaking capabilities.

Organize a chess team. This skill is very important for developing cognitive abilities. Why not start a team that travels throughout the community competing against other children? Competition is healthy for developing positive self-esteem.

Create a hobby. What is your passion relating to your hobby? Whatever it is, pursue it diligently and invite African Americans to join you.

Interacting cross-culturally doesn't have to be burdensome. Just find out what you are interested in doing and have us join you. It is as simple as that.

Chapter Twelve

On Your Mark, Get Ready, Get Set, Go

We know that in the twenty-first century racism is just as blatant as it was two hundred years ago. The practice of discrimination is no longer a covert operation. It persists in all segments of society—the corporate boardrooms, media, educational systems, economics, social structures, institutions and virtually anywhere else there are people. It is very pervasive and has cumulative effects.

Is there any hope?

Sure there is! With God all things are possible. What can we do to ensure that our grandchildren will have a better future concerning race relations? The only institution in the world that can assist us is the church, and just as churches and pastors were instrumental in bringing change through the Civil Rights Movement, the church is very capable of assisting us in reconciling cross-culturally. There are several suggestions the church can take to launch a movement in this country that would spark a national revival that would heal our land. These include:

Desegregating the local churches. Instead of setting up different camps on Sunday morning where the African Americans worship in one place, and the Hispanics, Asians, and Caucasians worship in other places, how about worshipping together? We need to start right now extending invitations to other cultures to sit right next to us as we worship. If we are to be in fellowship cross-culturally, we will need to be in constant dialogue. We need to discover why they don't attend our church, and what we can do to encourage their retention. We also need to partner with them in efforts to understand how we can facilitate their spiritual growth.

We need to organize a summit. We need to come together in the community at least monthly to iron out our differences. In order to reconcile we need to sit down at the table and reason together. We need to provide a friendly atmosphere where each side can communicate their specific needs. Many times conflict occurs because of miscommunication. Just like in a marriage relationship, your spouse cannot meet your needs unless you verbally communicate them. Even at that there is a possibility your words could be misinterpreted. We need to clearly speak what is on our minds. For example, if you're Caucasian and you are out to dinner with a group of African Americans, and someone makes a rash comment about the Hispanic waiter and all the African Americans laugh, you need to clearly communicate your disapproval. Not only by not laughing, but you can also say to the individual, "I really don't think that was an appropriate comment."

We also need to clarify the best strategy for assisting us with understanding our brother's or sister's plight. We have to be willing to make a lifetime commitment to establishing a deeper relationship with them. We have to discern what their primary concerns are and address them as efficiently as possible. Of course perfection is not always attainable in these instances, but as Christ followers we are expected to pursue reconciliation with diligence and excellence.

Stay true to your mission statement. Before you begin your journey to reconcile cross-culturally, you need to have some idea what your goals and objectives are relating to this. Are you motivated out of a sense of duty or obligation? Do you want to reconcile because it is politically correct? Or are you feeling guilty over the actions of your ancestors? If you are on this journey for any of the above reasons, do us all a favor: Stop right now! In the long run you will do more harm to us than good if you are simply going through the actions.

We should be on this journey because of Whose we are. Remember we are bought with a high price. The fear of our Lord should be one of our primary motivators. We should desire reconciliation because it is at the heart of our Lord. In our efforts to please Him, we should sacrifice whatever inconvenience we will experience for the greatest good. Our mission should not be impossible concerning reconciling. We all need to begin with a mission statement that will give us directions for our journey.

Please take a few minutes to write out a mission statement.

Example: I, Kandis Heckler, hereby agree to teach racial reconciliation throughout the world as often as humanly possible to effect positive change in our society. My only motivation is because of who Jesus Christ is and what He did for me on the cross at Calvary. I plan on sending this resource to church groups worldwide at my expense and will commit to proactively setting aside some time on a monthly basis to serve the church in order to assist them in fulfilling their high calling in Jesus Christ.

Please write your own mission statement:

Allow the Lord to interrupt your plans. This is a very challenging commitment. How many of us get ahead of the Lord and literally plan our lives without consulting Him? I have never been one for waiting patiently for the Lord to move. I always felt He needed my help. The God who created the heavens and the earth in six days *doesn't* need my help. Eventually I figured out that I always ended up with Him directing my paths. Why not start out with Him initially? The book concept was nothing I was ever remotely interested in writing. I had my own plans. But how many of us know that when the Lord calls you to do something, you'd better do it!

We cannot allow the devil to steal our purpose. We are all created for one specific calling. We have a destiny to fulfill and a Lord to glorify. We cannot allow the devil to distract us from our legacy. Do you want all God has for you? I surely do. And when the devil tries to remind you of your past regarding your apathy, just remind him of his future. The devil loves it when we are in strife and in contention. He literally mocks our God when he sees that God's creation cannot dwell on the earth amicably. When we are indecisive and antagonistic, the demons are literally laughing at us. Do you know how powerful we can be as a nation if we were all united and on one accord? We could do some serious damage to the kingdom of darkness.

Remember reconciliation across racial lines and class systems was at the heart of Jesus Christ. Jesus established reconciliation as a characteristic His followers would embrace if they truly had a close, personal relationship with Him. He expects that if we say we love Him whom we have never seen, surely we can love our brothers and sisters who are different whom we see daily. Besides, if we in the church don't get this right, who will?

The church's response is to pray that God's will be done on earth as it is in heaven. And we all know there is no segregation in heaven. There are no "whites only" and "coloreds only" signs up there. In keeping this in mind, we need to set an example for the governmental, educational, social, and political systems to follow. The Acts 2 church responded to their community's needs. They didn't rely on the government. We must be willing to rise above our circumstances and lay aside all preconceived ideas about other groups of people. Are you a willing vessel? Are you ready to use your gifts, talents and resources to effect a change?

Spiritual Gifts Inventory

According to Romans 12:6-8, "We have different gifts, according to the grace given us, if a man's gift is prophesying, let him use it in proportion to his faith. If it is serving, let him serve; if it is teaching, let him teach; if it is encouraging, let him encourage; if it is contributing to the needs of others, let him give generously; if it is leadership, let him govern diligently; if it is showing mercy, let him do it cheerfully."

What are your spiritual gifts? Please list each one.

1.
2.
3.
4.
5.

Please take each gift and write one sentence on how you will use your gifts. Then write your plan of action for racing towards reconciliation.

Example:

Gift: Teaching—I have decided that I would teach this curriculum in my church and lead small group sessions.

Plan of Action: Beginning in two weeks, I will meet with church leadership and develop strategies on how we can begin to teach this curriculum church-wide.

Gift:

Plan of Action:

Gift:

Plan of Action:

Gift:

Plan of Action:

Gift:

Plan of Action:

Gift:

Plan of Action:

Whatever your gifts are, bring them to the table and lay them down and serve. A small investment in your time will produce great dividends for the kingdom of heaven. We never said racial reconciliation would be easy or cost-effective. Anything worthwhile requires personal sacrifice.

As a reconciliator you are called to a great task which may be met with persecution and trepidation. You may be mistreated, abused, misunderstood, misinterpreted and may very well be ostracized by your spouse, family, friends and church members. But just as Jesus Christ told His disciples in Matthew 10:14, "'If anyone will not welcome you or listen to your words, shake the dust off your feet when you leave that home or town.'"

Do the same. Don't waste your time. It took racist people years to develop their views and hatred. Not a chance you will be able to change them overnight. It just won't happen. Healing is a process. Remember when you first came to Christ? Did your sinful habits change overnight? NOT! Well, give them the same grace Jesus extended to you. We have to love them to our side. We have to first point them to Jesus and secondly allow the Holy Spirit's power, which richly dwells within us, to convict them. Just make sure your own house is in order first to enable the Lord to use you as a conduit for assisting them on their journey. We are all in this together.

If you're unsure about this whole process start off slowly. If you've never interacted with an African-American individual before, now would be the time to begin. I wouldn't necessarily propose you invite them over for dinner, not just yet. You are still in the infancy stage. Try to build a casual relationship over a cup of coffee first. Then as the friendship matures perhaps you can graduate to a more formal approach. Always use wisdom and exercise discernment. If you are lacking in these areas consult your spiritually mature friends. None of us would marry someone our family and friends didn't approve of.

Let me caution you. You know we have an Enemy who is very good at his job. He will pull all stops to discourage you. But don't give up. Try and try again. We all have different personalities. Sometimes the chemistry just isn't there. That individual may not live up to your expectations or you to theirs. And be careful not to ascribe a mere human component of sin to racism. Not all stressful relationships should be attributed to someone having a racist attitude. Don't forget we are all sinners saved by grace. If the relationship turns sour, move on to the next one. There are representatives of dysfunction in every culture.

We have to pour new wine into new wineskins. According to Matthew 9:16-17, "'No one sews a patch of unshrunk cloth on an old garment, for the patch will pull away from the garment, making the tear worse. Neither do men pour new wine into old wineskins. If they do, the skins will burst, the wine will run out and the wineskins will be ruined. No, they pour new wine into new wineskins, and both are preserved.'"

We in the African-American community are guilty of this. We have been holding on to traditions for generations. For as long as I can remember, my great-grandmother always served black-eyed peas every New Year. The tradition was passed down from her to my grandmother and to my mother. Well, being the rebel I am, one New Year day I decided that we would have barbecue chicken and ribs with potato salad and coleslaw. When everyone gathered for the meal, you would have thought I'd committed a crime when they realized we were not having black-eyed pea, greens and cornbread. I was an outcast the entire day. When I inquired about the hostility for breaking tradition, my relatives all stated that everything else in their lives is always fluctuating and the only stability they had was to hold on to certain holiday traditions. I decided the following year to return to the traditional meal plus have a different meal prepared for those who wanted a different menu. I guess you would say I was a conformist. But whatever it takes to place someone's needs above mine I am willing to do. Another vivid example of holding on to traditions occurred when I was attending my former African-American church. I recall Sunday after Sunday singing the same song. I remember the same deacon praying the same prayer and although the announcements varied each week, they were always spoken by the same sister and read at the same time like clockwork, every Sunday. Around the fifteenth year of the same routine, I asked the pastor why we always performed the same rituals Sunday after Sunday. His response was, "Because we've always done it this way."

If we are planning to reconcile we will have to sacrifice some of our old traditions, even if it means we have to sing worship songs that we don't like in order to accommodate the different members of our body. I've seen a church in Atlanta, Georgia that is racially mixed. They have at least six different choirs. Their members each week have a choice between classical style of worship, country, rock and roll, blues, contemporary, rap, and jazz. It's amazing to witness how they rotate these choirs in order to appeal to the needs of the congregation. (I know it's a lot of work, but isn't it worth it?)

The only caution here is you already know it is virtually impossible to be all things to all people. You are inevitably going to offend someone or inadvertently miss the mark. That is okay. All God requires is for us to be very intentional.

A second caution concerning doctrine and biblical traditions is we cannot compromise. The Word of God must stay the same.

Allow the Holy Spirit to convict you where you have fallen short and trust His power to change your views regarding African Americans. If the Lord can heal a drug-addicted individual, a murderer named Moses, and an adulterer named David, what is so hard about Him healing an individual with racist views? Isn't He the God of second chances, and third, fourth, fifth and so on?

The church has to step up to the plate. The church has to set the example first. Reconciliation has to be pursued feverishly from the pulpit. For years the church has been hesitant to stir up the hornet's nest because they are afraid they may get stung. Some churches worry about what may happen to their tithes and offerings if they make room for other ethnic groups to attend. When the church fails to recognize diversity and falters in providing solace to a downtrodden and brokenhearted group of people, they are nailing Jesus back to the cross. The church has to take an activist approach to achieving diversity. If we are truly in Christ we will never be guilty of being disunited with our brothers and sisters. God requires nothing less than for Christ followers to always take a stand for righteousness concerning racial reconciliation. We are the ecclesiastical, called out, the light of the world. This is not a governmental responsibility. It is the churches'. God is calling us to change our perception of others. He's trying to unite us here on earth first. There are going to be people from every tribe and nation sitting at Jesus's feet and singing in the heavenly chorus. Dress rehearsal starts down here first.

We must do a total surrendering of our self. We must transform our personalities from hostile to humble. Be intentional in diversifying. In order to reconcile we must take an active approach in hiring qualified African Americans for full-time ministry or in the corporate setting. There has to be a strategic plan for employing their services. I applaud Promise Keepers and other organizations, churches, social service agencies, political entities, corporations and educational institutions for their intentionally. Promise Keepers saw a need and intentionally hired African-American men to address the concerns of the organization. They are actively pursuing racial reconciliation in our community.

If we let our request be made known to God, He will honor our desires when they line up with His Word. Just make sure you seek His face concerning the individual. I know a church in my community that thought they were hearing from God concerning their choice of pastor. Needless to say the experience with him was very unfruitful.

Pray! God can raise up an African-American leader right out of the body. Pray! Observe them very carefully. Pray! Do they meet the Scriptural requirements of 1 Timothy 3:1-13? If they do, what are you waiting for?

Begin reconciliation with prayer and fasting. This is imperative if you want to receive all the Lord has for you concerning this journey. Ask for wisdom, guidance, direction and protection. Jesus often withdrew from the crowds to pray. He had to commune with His Father in order to gird His ministry. Our prayers should not involve telling God what our plans are. They should be us cooperating fully with His plans. This is spiritual warfare against the kingdom of God and His foes. The prince of the air is positioned to wage war against us. The only way to deactivate his power is to pray without ceasing.

Fasting should also be an integral part of your monthly routine. I always fast prior to any speaking commitments. First of all, it gets the Lord's attention. When you are willing to crucify the desires of your flesh it communicates a sense of urgency. He can't resist helping you when you sacrifice like that. Secondly, it clears my mind, it gives me increased concentration and gives me unhindered communion with the Lord. In that time I am able to petition His throne for wisdom concerning the people I will be ministering to.

Reconciliation is spiritual warfare. Any time you engage in battle, it is wise for you to not only petition the throne on another's behalf, but you also need an intercessor to petition the throne on your behalf. You have to bathe, shower and clothe yourself with prayer daily for the challenges ahead of you. Set aside prayer and devotional time as a part of your morning, afternoon or evening routine. We have to pray for protection against the fiery darts of the Evil One. We need a burning, passionate desire for prayer.

We have to walk by faith and not by sight. In order for our attempts at reconciliation to be effective we must walk in the Spirit, not in the natural. In order for us to bear any good fruit, we must not only think out of the box but we will have to step outside it also. We have to operate in faith because faith without works is dead. We need to show the world that we Christians have it together concerning loving one another, or at least show them we are trying. Let's not give the devil any more fuel for the fire. For centuries he has done a good job keeping us all isolated from one another. The reason for this is because he realizes how much power will come through the body of Jesus Christ if we all unite. The devil wants to block our blessings because he knows what unity can bring. We would literally be able to rule this sinful world. There would be revival in the land once the church gets reconciliation right. We will give the devil a run for his money.

Walking by faith requires that we eliminate any sense of comfort. We cannot judge our standards rationally. Even when it seems foolish to enter a crime-infested neighborhood in an attempt to reconcile cross-culturally, we need to go for it. Just exercise wisdom while you are there. The same Lord that called you to enter that neighborhood will be the same God who protects you.

I can recall an experience when I was ministering in a public housing project. As I was pursuing a teenage mom to introduce Christ to her, we walked right into a pharmaceutical transaction (drug dealing). Now the foolish thing would have been for me to try and witness to those men who were obviously in more need of Jesus Christ than she was. The Holy Spirit quickened me and told me to get out of there as quickly as possible. The moral of the story is to listen to the Lord. I asked the woman if she wanted to hang out on the playground. A few minutes later she prayed to receive Christ.

When the Lord called me to minister there I had to trust He would protect me. Obedience is better than sacrifice even if it means risking your life. Look at Noah's example in the Old Testament. The Lord instructed him to build an ark because rain was coming. And although Noah had never seen rain in his life, he took God at His Word, even though it didn't rain until one hundred years later. Noah and his family were spared. Despite the persecution of the community Noah stayed true to God's command. Whatever God calls you to do He will equip you to do. In light of all eternity, we have to trust God and pursue racial reconciliation with reckless abandon.

In order to reconcile we have to die to the law and the former ways of doing things. You cannot hold on to the law and live for God at the same time. If your company has never done business with an African-American individual, aren't you about due? Galatians 2:19 states, "For through the law I died to the law so that I might live for God." According to this passage you are still holding on to the law. Die to your flesh and the old customs and take the risk of economically empowering someone outside your comfortable circle. There will inevitably be issues and offenses when you merge two people from different perspectives. Don't believe me, ask your spouse. Brace yourself for conflicts. You may even have your theology challenged.

I will never forget my experiences working with juvenile delinquents. They taught me a lot about life. I learned from them that society sets standards of right and wrong based on the majority's values. For example, in some cultures lying is perfectly acceptable for the greater good. For instance, you may have a man who was recently paroled. Well, in order to stay out of jail one of the conditions is full time employment.

To obtain employment you have to complete an application. On the application form it asks if you've been a convicted felon. In order for this ex-felon to get a job, he must lie. My point is, in order to racially reconcile you may have to give up your moral convictions long enough to identify with the individual. I am not suggesting you compromise your integrity. I am just saying although you have reasons for your position, rest from your desire to stand in judgment of another individual who is trying to survive. Remember the truth can always be measured against the Word of God. Look at the situation from all perspectives and when in doubt call on the Holy Spirit.

Become a student of racial reconciliation. Ignorance is not bliss in this situation. Study African Americans to find out what makes us tick. Spend quality time with us. As a student you are not trying to change our culture. You are just trying to understand it. Make it a point to embrace the customs by listening to our music, reading books authored by us, traveling to places we reside in, and tasting our food. Ensure that your children are active participants as well. They need a head start. Haven't you heard that those who help the oppressed honor God? What are you waiting for?

We have to renew our minds. According to Romans 12:2, "Do not conform any longer to the pattern of this world, but be transformed by the renewing of your mind. Then you will be able to test and approve what God's will is—his good, pleasing and perfect will." In order to renew your mind you have to break the yoke of bondage in your heart. The first step would be to acknowledge your sin, the second step is to repent, which is an actual turning away from the transgression, and the third step is to embrace a commitment to effect a change.

Psalm 139:23 says, "Search me, O God, and know my heart; test me and know my anxious thoughts. See if there is any offensive way in me, and lead me in the way everlasting."

In order to renew our minds, regeneration has to occur. We must literally reprogram ourselves. During the Trent Lott controversy several years ago, I remember hearing him making comments about how he was raised as a segregationist by his parents. He implied, what should we expect if he was raised like this? There is validity to his comment. However, there are people in our society who were horrifically abused as children and somehow grew up to be non-abusers. There are also those individuals raised by dysfunctional parents who escaped the ravages of their parents' sins. Psychology textbooks are filled with examples of drug- and alcohol-addicted parents whose children grew up to be moral and law-abiding citizens. So Mr. Lott's argument holds no weight. Personally, I felt he shouldn't have stepped down. I'd rather deal with an overt racist than a covert one. At least I can recognize my enemy and hold him accountable for his or her actions. Trent Lott would have probably been more effective and advocated on our behalf because he was being watched by an entire nation.

Renewing of the mind also involves our ability to control our thought life. Second Corinthians 10:3-5 states, "For though we live in the world, we do not wage war as the world does. The weapons we fight with are not the weapons of the world. On the contrary, they have divine power to demolish strongholds. We demolish arguments and every pretension that sets itself up against the knowledge of God, and we take captive every thought to make it obedient to Christ."

In capturing every thought we have a choice to entertain negative thoughts or positive ones. The devil is a deceiver who desperately tries to control our minds. He places thoughts in our minds that we instantly replay over and over again. Have you allowed thoughts of offense, pain, hurt, low self-esteem, failure and regrets to permeate your very existence? Negative thoughts are not from the Lord. As Christ followers we are more than conquers. When we are faced with defeat we need to evict thoughts of depression, hopelessness, anger, anxiety, self-pity or worry from our minds. We can overcome these with faith, the Word of God and prayer.

One of the tricks the Enemy uses is deception. He enjoys distorting the truth. Ever since Adam and Eve were in the garden he tried to contradict the Word of God. He asked Eve, "Did God really say that?" Satan made them feel like God was depriving them of something good. When your thoughts contradict God's Word the devil is setting you up big time. There is absolutely no truth in him. He's the father of lies. When we resist him he will flee.

According to Philippians 2:5, "Your attitude should be the same as that of Christ Jesus." And we all know that His mind and heart were pure. Every thought or action He performed was good.

Every sin we conceive is from a thought. If we don't restrain each thought, the devil controls our mind. That's why television can be hazardous to our health. We need to change the radio stations we are listening to, and any type of music that is not God honoring needs to be incinerated. Our computer programs should blot out explicit material on the Internet. Remember whatever diet you feed your spirit will determine how healthy you will be. I liken sin to a computer program, garbage in means garbage out. When we nourish our souls with the Word of God, listen to worship music, have a devotional time and bathe ourselves in prayer, we exterminate the devil's presence in our lives.

The next time we allow the devil to infiltrate our thoughts like, "This reconciliation thing is such a waste of my time. Those people aren't going to change anyway, so what's the point?" tell the devil, "I have the mind of Christ, so leave me alone." Refuse him admission to your thought life. Whenever he is surfing through your mind, change the channel. Romans 8:6-8 tells us, "The mind of sinful man is death, but the mind controlled by the Spirit is life and peace; the sinful mind is hostile to God. It does not submit to God's law, nor can it do so. Those controlled by the sinful nature cannot please God." In reconciling cross-culturally, if we are controlled by any other motives such as guilt, concern for what other people think, because it is the politically correct thing to do, or for selfish gain, we cannot please God. There is absolutely no need for you to continue on your journey, because all of your attempts will be in vain.

That is why the Scripture reference in James 1:13-15 is so powerful. It states, "When tempted, no one should say, 'God is tempting me.' For God cannot be tempted by evil, nor does he tempt anyone; but each one is tempted when, by his own evil desire, he is dragged away and enticed. Then, after desire has conceived, it gives birth to sin; and sin, when it is full-grown, gives birth to death." You see sin is a process. Desire occurs, then it gives birth to sin, and sin develops and gives birth to death. Same with your thought life. Don't let it mature past the conception stage. For example, men being as visual as they are have a difficult time controlling their lustful desires. Just one thought could entertain a man all afternoon.

So the next time a negative thought flashes across your mind about another culture, try this exercise: sing or even pray while your mind is in overdrive. You will be surprised by how that thought changes. Sometimes we need to discern which thoughts to entertain and which to release. The way to judge those is to always measure your thoughts against God's Word. If your thought is saying, "That black homeless person over there needs to get a job because nothing is free in this world," your thoughts are negative. Do you really know their entire situation? What does the Word say about homeless people? I recall reading a Scripture reference that says, ""'For I was hungry and you gave me nothing to eat, I was thirsty and you gave me nothing to drink, I was a stranger and you did not invite me in, I needed clothes and you did not clothe me, I was sick and in prison and you did not look after me." They also will answer, "Lord, when did we see you hungry or thirsty or a stranger or needing clothes or sick or in prison, and did not help you?" He will reply, "I tell you the truth, whatever you did not do for one of the least of these, you did not do for me." Then they will go away to eternal punishment, but the righteous to eternal life.'"

Renewing the mind also involves searching the Scripture for what the Word of God says concerning racial reconciliation. When I was convicted of my sin of not obeying those in authority over me whole-heartily, I immediately began to work on changing. My first inclination was to hire a psychologist to talk me out of it. My second option was to hire an exorcist. My third option was to listen to tapes on submission. None of these techniques were necessary. Like Jesus told Martha in Luke 10:41, "'Martha, Martha...you are worried and upset about many things, but only one thing is needed. Mary has chosen what is better, and it will not be taken away from her.'" Martha chose to sit at the feet of Jesus. I chose to learn submission by sitting at the feet of my Savior.

As I fasted and prayed He told me to write out every Scripture verse relating to submission in the Bible. He told me to post them throughout my home. He also instructed me to confess daily what I was believing Him for, to listen to worship music relating to surrender, and to praise Him for the victory even before I saw it.

After about one week of following His directions, I felt a heavy burden lift from my shoulders. The major tug-of-war battles seemed to dissipate immediately, and I began to experience a total peace with God. At this writing I am not yet fully submitted, but thank God I am on my way.

Daily prayer and confession is the most effective technique for renewing the mind. For example, if you have something against your brother or sister because of their membership to a certain race, you need to acknowledge this sin. You might say, "Lord, I am trying to love my brother and sister cross-culturally. But because of the way I was raised I am having a difficult time with this." The second step would be to repent. "Lord, I am sorry, I clearly know this is not your design for men to live amongst men in strife, anger and contention. I know racism is clearly not your way. I am to live peaceably with all men. So please allow your Holy Spirit's power to richly engulf me. Make me and mold me into the man or woman of God you intended for me to be. I am relying on you totally for the change in my life. I am nothing without you, Lord. I am an heir of Abraham according to your promises, and I want everything you have for me. So, Lord, anoint me with oil. Don't hold anything back from me. Please forgive me of all my trespasses. I thank you that I am more than a conquer and I can do all things through you who strengthens me. So right now I call on your precious name to equip me and enable me to love my brother and sister cross-culturally. I want all of my thoughts to be your thoughts and all my ways to be your ways. Thank you, Lord, in advance for the victory. Amen."

Please write out your own prayer and place it in a place where you can see it on a daily basis:

Search the Scriptures for five passages that speak of racial reconciliation and write them down. Commit them to memory.

1.
2.
3.
4.
5.

In order to effect change dramatically in your life concerning reconciliation, you will also need to make daily confessions. Please write down a simple confession you intend to say daily to assist you with your race towards reconciliation.

My daily confession is: Lord, I thank you that you have commissioned me to fulfill your calling in the area of racial reconciliation. I fully acknowledge that I am a sinful human being who is redeemed by your precious blood shed on the cross at Calvary. I ask for your forgiveness for all my sins. I welcome your will for my life. I am joining you in the work you have for me. I present my body as a willing, living and consecrated vessel to be used for your glory. I release you to change me, to conform me to your image. Lord, I lay down my life for you in this area and surrender my total will to you. I am reconciled first to you and secondly to my brothers and sisters cross-culturally. I am at peace with all men. I celebrate each one of their differences, knowing that ultimately we are all one in you. Father, open my mind and enlarge my heart towards them. Thank you for dying on the cross to reconcile yourself to us. And now I ask for you to create in me a clean heart and renew a steadfast spirit within me as I race towards reconciliation. Amen.

Give the Lord the glory when reconciliation occurs. Give Him the praise because we know we could never achieve this goal on our own. It is only through the Holy Spirit's working power that we could effect this type of change in an individual's life. So give Him the glory! Trust Him with more victories as you acknowledge Him as the Victor.

A final word to individuals, churches and organizations who are striving daily to reconcile cross-culturally to their brothers and sisters in Christ: Keep up the good work! God is very pleased with your efforts! "Let us not become weary in doing good, for at the proper time we will reap a harvest if we do not give up" (Galatians 6:9).

You did it! You made it! Congratulations! Thank you for racing towards reconciliation with me. I pray this workshop whets your appetite and you will have a passionate desire to explore this issue even further.

Remember we are all in this together. According to Philippians 2:1-2, "If you have any encouragement from being united with Christ, if any comfort from his love, if any fellowship with the Spirit, if any tenderness and compassion, then make my joy complete by being like-minded, having the same love, being one in spirit and purpose." We have to be one in spirit with the same goals in order to combat racism. There needs to be a unity, a like-mindedness to serve Christ together with our fellow man. It involves all of us using our different gifts in the body to effect change.

As we seek to dwell in this unity, God will be in the midst of us. He will pour out His blessings on all of our attempts at reconciling cross-culturally. He will be glorified at the efforts we put forth on our brothers' and sisters' behalves. There's no greater reward for those who demonstrate God's character in their life.

Remember, it was only one color of blood shed for us all. Are you prepared to lay down your life for a friend? If you answered yes, then you're on your way. ***On your mark, get ready, get set, go!***

"Therefore, since we are surrounded by such a great cloud of witnesses, let us throw off everything that hinders and the sin that so easily entangles, and let us run with perseverance the race marked out for us."

-Hebrews 12:1

Answer Key

For the answers to all the questions in this book please dialogue with your small groups. If that doesn't work, contact the author at agapeproductions@sbcglobal.net.

Bibliography

Webster's New World Dictionary, Second Edition (1982) New York: Simon & Schuster Inc.

To be aware of the need for racial reconciliation and to not do anything about it is worse than racism itself.

We waste a lot of time on trying to cure racism. Instead we should try to prevent the illness through multicultural education.

Our greatest fears concerning racial reconciliation is conceived out of ignorance. But once we give birth to the truth the Lord will hold us accountable for our actions.

Neutrality is advantageous to the oppressor. Silence is an indictment in the crime of racism, and anyone who doesn't speak against it should be charged as an accessory.

When we become intentional in bonding all races together, and acknowledging the masterful work of an omnipotent Creator. We will understand our purposes for living.

We must divorce ourselves from cynicism in relation to racial reconciliation because it is incompatible with the marriage we have with Jesus Christ.

Kandis Heckler

www.ingramcontent.com/pod-product-compliance
Lightning Source LLC
LaVergne TN
LVHW061223100826
845148LV00004B/842